Llamas on the Trail
A Packer's Guide

David Harmon and Amy S. Rubin
Drawings by Nancy Diane Russell

Mountain Press Publishing Company
Missoula, Montana
1992

Library of Congress Cataloging-in-Publication Data

Harmon, David, 1961-
    Llamas on the trail :   a packer's guide   /   David Harmon and Amy S.
Rubin ;   drawings by Nancy Diane Russell.
        p.   cm.
    Includes bibliographical references and index.
    ISBN 0-87842-251-X : $15.00
    1. Llama pack camping.   2. Llamas.   I. Rubin, Amy S., 1961-
II. Title.
GV199.75.H37   1992   92-35364
796.54—dc20   CIP

Mountain Press Publishing Company
P.O. Box 2399
Missoula, Montana 59806

To Black-Eyed-Jack our first and best pack llama; and to our families who didn't laugh too much when we told them we were moving to Montana and going into the llama business.

Table of Contents

Acknowledgements

This book got its start through the open-mindedness of certain faculty members at the University of Montana. Thanks to Tom Roy, Steve Cole, Steve McCool, and Chris Field for listening to Dave explain the need for a professional paper about packing with llamas.

Some of the material in this book previously appeared in *Llama Life*, a newspaper serving the llama community, published in Durango, Colorado.

Also thanks to Marvin and Joy Rubin for their support from the very beginning, for their thoughtful editorial comments, and for the generous gift that allowed us to travel to South America. Thank you to Marvin for many of the photos taken on the trail.

We greatly appreciate the editorial comments of Naomi Rubin and Mary Thorndike and the efforts of the staff at Mountain Press for taking on this project and seeing it through to completion.

To all the llama owners who have so willingly shared their time, knowledge, and enthusiasm, thank you.

Thanks to Pocahontas the llama for letting us put the halter on five times so we could get just the right photograph.

And lastly, thanks to all our pack llamas, our "Speechless Brothers," who work so skillfully and without argument, and willingly share centuries of accumulated packing experience with us newcomers.

Lloving your llama.

Preface

We started raising and training llamas in 1986, originally because of their gentle nature and ease of maintenance. However, it took only one pack trip, with the llamas carrying all the supplies, to convince us that llamas could serve an important function beyond looking pretty. Ever since that first season we have spent our Montana summers high in the mountains with our pack string of much-loved llamas.

A few years ago, when only a small number of people traveled into the backcountry with llamas, it would have seemed ridiculous to write a book on packing with llamas. However, every year more people realize the benefits of packing with these exotic animals. Part of the initiative to write this book came from our wish that we had a book like this one when we first started packing with llamas. We learned what we could from other llama packers and from what little we could find to read, but mostly we learned from the llamas themselves and through trial and error.

Our love of wildlands provided another motivation to write this book. Llamas are unique companions that leave less of a mark in the wilderness than other traditional pack stock. Their full potential as low-impact stock animals is realized, however, only when used correctly. You will find many ideas for minimum impact backcountry travel throughout this book, and we hope you will take them to heart.

We have assembled here the knowledge we have accumulated over the past years of packing with llamas. Some of the ideas are our own, some are the ideas of friends and fellow packers. Many of the concepts and techniques are simply what we found works best for us. You should not shy from trying a variation on our themes—you could very well improve on our methods. When you do find a better way, share the information with others.

This book is for anyone interested in llama packing. For those folks considering buying a llama, we cover all the basics: from selecting a good pack llama to facilities needed before bringing the llama home. For people who already pack with llamas, this book will provide techniques and ideas to make trips easier, safer, and more enjoyable. If you are considering spending your vacation time on a commercial llama pack trip, this book will provide insight into the nature and history of the llama to make your trip more enjoyable.

When we cannot be out packing with our llamas we take them in parades, to the county fair, to nursing homes, to story-hour at the library, and on walks in the neighborhood. We have even taken them Christmas caroling. If you check around you will probably find llama owners in your area, and maybe even some in your neighborhood. Check with a vet or feed store for names of owners, and call to make an appointment to see their llamas. Llama owners will usually welcome visitors, and share their knowledge willingly.

Llamas roam among the ruins at Machu Picchu, the lost city of the Incas.

– 1 –

LLAMAS
Past and Present

Llamas from What?

In order to understand today's llama, we'll take a look at where the llama came from and how it evolved and changed over its long history.

Llamas and camels belong to the same family and are related in the same way foxes and wolves are related. If you were to observe a camel and a llama in the same pen, their close relationship would become apparent. Large eyes and long eyelashes would provide the first clue. Other similar features include the split in the front of the upper lip, the long neck, and large, rounded feet.

Kids, with their keen observational skills, will usually pick up the similarities between llamas and camels. One summer we accompanied two of our llamas in a local parade. All along the parade route we heard excited children saying, "Look! Camels!" and then an adult voice saying, "No, those are llamas."

The family camilidae, which includes llamas and camels, is divided into two subgroups, called genera. One genus, called Camelus, the

true camels, includes two species—the one-humped dromedary or Asian camel and the two-humped Bactrian camel of Mongolia. The other genus of the family camilidae, Lama (note the spelling with only one "L"), has four species which are all found in South America. The four species of the genus Lama include the guanaco, the vicuña, the alpaca, and the llama—that's the two-"L" llama which this book is about. The guanaco and the vicuña both roam free and wild in the mountains of South America, while the alpaca and llama are domesticated species. Ancient peoples may have domesticated the alpaca and llama from the two wild species.

The guanaco reaches a similar size as the llama, yet always has so-called "wild-type" coloration similar to that of a white-tailed deer—light on the belly and the inside of its legs and brown elsewhere. Occasionally llamas display this same "wild-type" coloration.

The other wild relative of the llama, the vicuña, is much smaller and has an extremely fine fleece. In Incan times, only high priests

1

were allowed to wear vicuña-fiber clothing. More recently, the fleece of the vicuña commanded a high price on international markets. But vicuñas are wild animals, making it difficult to catch them and shear their fleece, so the animals were often killed for their pelts. During the 1960s and 1970s, illegal killing pushed the vicuña to the brink of extinction. Although the vicuña is still listed as an endangered species, the South American governments have controlled the poaching, and the vicuña population is recovering.

Captive vicuña, Cuzco, Peru. In the times of the Incas only high priests were allowed to wear garments made from the fine vicuña wool.

The alpaca is a smaller, extremely woolly version of the llama. Domesticated but too small to carry heavy loads, alpacas are raised for their heavy coats of long fine wool and in South America for their meat.

Lamas (guanacos, vicuñas, alpacas, and llamas) and camels share a long history of evolution that began right here in North America. Modern camels and lamas came from the same ancient camelian stock that roamed the plains of central North America 40 to 45 million years ago. Three million years ago, some of these ancient camels migrated from North America to Asia via a small strip of land, called the Beringia Land Bridge, that once connected present day Alaska to the Soviet Union. This group traveled farther west across Asia and evolved into the dromedary and the Bactrian camels.

Another group of ancient camels turned south and migrated across the Panamanian Land Bridge into South America. This second group of animals evolved into the modern genus Lama, with its four associated species. Remains from these ancestors of the llama have been found right here in our home state of Montana. So don't let anyone tell you llamas are exotic animals and don't belong in North America. They got their start right here millions of years ago.

The camel family's long history has provided them ample time to evolve and adapt. Over the

With their fine coats of wool, alpacas are gaining popularity in the United States.

Alpacas are the smaller, woollier cousin to the llama.

years, as these animals were forced to survive in increasingly hostile environments, their bodies changed to meet the challenge. For example, today's camels have long, fine eyelashes and a secondary eyelid that protect the eye from blowing sand. Out of necessity, camels have also adapted to going for weeks without water. In order to walk on the soft desert sand, the camel developed a wide, flat, two-toed foot that acts as a snowshoe, distributing the weight over a large surface area. The pad on the bottom of the foot allows the camel to withstand the scorching heat of hot desert sands.

Members of the genus lama share some but not all of the camel's adaptations. Lamas have long eyelashes, an additional eyelid, and wide feet; however, lamas can go only a short time without water. Nevertheless, lamas experienced special modifications of their own that enable them to survive in the cold, harsh, high mountain environment of the South American Andes.

Llamas are one of the oldest domesticated species in the world. For over 5,000 years they have transported goods across the rugged Andes mountains of South America. The Incas, who flourished from 1200 A.D. until the Spanish

Pre-Columbian pictographs of llamas in Peru show their early domestication by the Incas.

Conquistadors arrived in 1532, selectively bred llamas for this purpose. The animals also provided meat, milk, and wool, and some speculate that llamas played a role in Incan religion as sacrificial animals.

When the Spaniards arrived, the Incan empire stretched over 2,500 miles from north to south. By far the most important role of the llama was transporting the Incas' potatoes, grown high in the Andes, down to the lower elevations where they could trade for corn and other wares. At the height of the Incan empire, caravans of between 1,000 and 2,000 llamas carrying between 30 and 60 tons of goods traversed the mountains. The Incas constructed vast stone monuments, terraced entire mountainsides, and built foundations using enormous stones that were quarried far from the building sites. It is not known exactly how the Incas managed to transport the stones from the quarry sites up to the building sites in the mountains, but llamas surely assisted in some way.

When the Spaniards invaded Peru, they destroyed much of the Incan empire in their quest for gold. Since llamas served an integral role in the Inca culture, the Spaniards destroyed vast breeding herds, as well as brutally killing Inca people, and destroying what they could of Incan cities and villages. However, because of

An alpaca grazes on the low protein forage of the Peruvian altiplano.

the size of the foundation stones used by the Incas and the precision with which the stones were fitted together, the Spaniards were unable to obliterate Incan structures. In fact, even today many of the highland cities and villages rise from these ancient Incan foundations.

After conquering the Incas, the Spaniards introduced their domestic cattle, horses, goats, and sheep. These animals received the best grazing lands, while llamas and alpacas were relegated to the less-productive, higher, mountain terrain. Although they transported minerals out of the mountains for the Spaniards, llamas never again attained the large populations or importance of the pre-Spanish period.

However, llamas still play a vital role in the lives of the highlanders of Peru, Bolivia, and Chile. We had the good fortune to spend ten weeks in South America during the winter (summer in South America) of 1990-1991. We saw many llamas in the high, remote altiplano of Peru and Bolivia. In urban areas, the automobile has replaced the llama for transporting goods—although in towns we occasionally saw a group of several llamas loaded with supplies bound for market.

Despite Peru's political and economic turmoil, life in the high, remote regions of the country remains very much the same as it was before the Spaniards arrived. In the upper regions of Peru, at altitudes of over 12,000 feet, the cows and sheep introduced by the Spaniards cannot thrive. Llamas and alpacas, however, subsist very well on the low-protein forage available at these altitudes and provide an excellent source of meat for the native people.

Meat from llamas is low in cholesterol, low in fat, and high in protein. One study shows llama meat as almost twenty percent higher in protein than beef. The ability of the llamas to subsist on practically nothing, yet produce high protein meat, makes them an invaluable asset to these native people.

The people in the country, the campesinos, maintain a traditional relationship with the llama. One remote village we visited in the high dry mountains of Peru depends on the llama for survival. Because only the wealthiest people can afford a vehicle, the llama and an occasional donkey offer the only means of transporting these people's supplies over the long, twelve-mile trip to the closest town. Few trees or woody shrubs grow in this area of the Andes, so the villagers burn dried llama dung as a source of heat. The villagers make much of their outer clothing, such as woven ponchos and knitted sweaters, plus their ropes (called sogas) out of llama wool. These South American natives rely on the llama today, much as North American natives depended upon the buffalo in the past.

Peruvian woman spins llama wool using a traditional drop spindle.

Llamas in North America

In the 1930s, Peru prohibited the export of its national animal, the llama. Bolivia soon followed suit. At about the same time, the United States and Canada restricted importation of camelids (llamas, alpacas, and vicuñas) from South American countries to prevent the spread of diseases, namely foot-and-mouth disease.

When importations were halted, only a few llamas lived in North America, mostly in zoos. The Catskill Game Farm in Catskill, New York, and William Randolph Hearst, wealthy publisher and newspaper magnate, owned private herds of less than 100 animals. Hearst imported llamas as novelty animals for his large estate in California. After Hearst's death in 1951, many of his llamas were sent to the Catskill Game Farm. Almost all the llamas in the United States and Canada today are descendants of these pre-World War II imports.

In 1992, about 30,000 llamas lived in the United States. (This figure is based on projections made by the International Lama Registry from the 22,000 registered female llamas in 1992, assuming a female/male ratio of 10/9. "Llama Life," Vol. 21, Spring 1992, page 14, D. Graham.) In contrast, there were over a million llamas in Peru, and over three million alpacas, the woolly cousin to the llama. However, the number of llamas and alpacas in Peru and other South American countries has declined significantly over the past 20 years because of development and changes in rural lifestyle.

In the past ten years, a few groups of approximately 100 llamas and alpacas were imported into the United States from Chile and Bolivia. Since these llamas represented new genetic lines they sold for astronomical prices, often upwards of $50,000. Despite a lengthy quarantine period, these recent importations have created great controversy in the livestock and llama industries. It is questionable whether quarantining llamas sufficiently protects against diseases such as tuberculosis (TB) and foot-and-mouth disease (FMD), which are common in South America.

In the summer of 1990, the Canadian government closed its borders to all llama importation after animals from Europe, which had tested negative for TB, later developed the disease. At this time, no reliable test exists to detect the presence of FMD or TB in llamas that carry the disease but do not show symptoms.

Today's Llama Market

The ban on importing camelids from South America has limited the number of breeding females and, consequently, the number of young llamas produced each year in North America. In 1980, about 350 female llama babies were born in the United States. Throughout the 1980s the demand for llamas far exceeded the supply, causing the price of llamas, especially breeding females, to rise dramatically. In 1989, around 3,000 female llamas were born in the United States. Many breeders opted to keep their young females to increase their herds, further tightening the market for female llamas. Such a limited supply of breeding females inflated prices even more.

In 1978 people paid $1,500 for a breeding pair. By the early 1980s the price had jumped to $3,000 for a young female llama, and by 1989 the price of a young female averaged $8,000. Auctions set record prices of $175,000 in 1989 for a highly promoted stud and $170,000 for a female bred to that stud. (These prices were set in October, 1989, at the Celebrity Llama Sale in Oklahoma City. At that sale, a group of people from Montana and California paid $175,000 for a male stud llama named Catman, sold by Great Northern Llama Company of Columbia Falls, Montana, and an Oregon llama ranch paid a record price of $170,000 for a female llama named Mirabelle, bred by Taylor Llamas of Bozeman, Montana.)

The high-priced woolly llamas still sell well at auction, attracting the attention of the high-rolling investors and movie stars. But many people are purposely moving away from the showier woolly llama, and instead breeding larger, short-wool llamas as breeding stock and pack llamas. Because of their reproductive capabilities, female llamas still sell for four or five times more than males, but many good packing or pet male llamas are available and affordable. You can find these llamas at lower prices by visiting local llama farms and ranches.

Female crias, such as little Belle Starr, shown here with her mother, Pocahontas, fetch top dollar in today's llama market.

Why Llamas?

Our first extended exposure to llamas was in 1986 when we visited a friend of a friend in Colorado who owned llamas. The agreement was we could stay at his place if we helped train Blaze, a large adult male llama, to pull a cart with two dogs in the driver's seat. We approached the project tentatively, but quickly learned that llamas are quite forgiving, very gentle, and extremely intelligent. Three days later Blaze was pulling the cart, and we were convinced that someday we would own one of these creatures.

Llamas have recently gained enormous popularity in North America. Some llama enthusiasts invest in high-priced breeding stock; others enjoy llamas as pets, wool producers, pack animals, or enlist them to protect sheep from marauding dogs and coyotes. Because llamas have a gentle and shy nature, do not bite, rarely kick, and are easy to handle, they make ideal pets. Naturally housebroken, llamas can visit indoors, and they can be trained to pull a cart or carry small children on their backs. They require only simple, inexpensive fencing and

A volunteer demonstrates hand spinning with llama wool in southern Maine. Llama wool is especially soft.

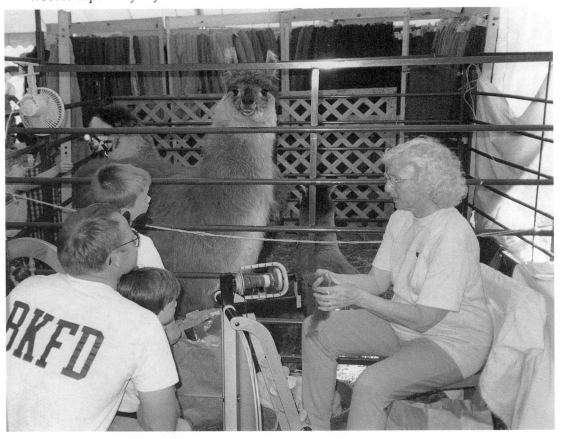

housing, a few acres, and minimal daily maintenance.

Although llamas do not yield the quantity of wool that their alpaca cousins produce, the excellent quality of llama wool attracts hand-spinners. The llama owner can either shear the animal or wait for the llama to molt, which happens every few years, and brush out three or more pounds of good wool.

When hiking with llamas one still has the satisfaction of hiking, not riding, all day—but without the extra burden of a heavy pack. Pack llamas fill the niche between the horse packer and the backpacker. As backpackers age, have children, or suffer an injury, they begin to see llamas as an alternative to carrying a heavy pack. Many young adults give up backpacking when they have children because they cannot carry a child and all their supplies into the backcountry. Llamas allow parents to travel with small children, while the pack animal carries the supplies. Some folks who are intimidated by the size of a horse and the perceived risk of injury see the llama as a safe means of getting themselves and their supplies into the backcountry.

Male llamas priced between $500 and $1,500 make excellent pack animals. Since packing into the backcountry entails some risk of injury to the llama, people generally leave their more

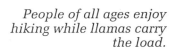
People of all ages enjoy hiking while llamas carry the load.

valuable female llamas at home. Besides, the females are usually pregnant or nursing and thus not available for packing.

During the summer months we offer guided backcountry excursions into the mountains of western Montana. Most of the people we take out have no prior backcountry experience. With the llamas carrying the load, we are able to provide a rather luxurious camping trip. After four days of tranquility, we send people home with a greater appreciation for the importance of protecting wildlands. One guest we will never forget was a woman who assured us that she had been camping before, but never overnight. We are still trying to figure that one out.

While on that trip she discovered the stars, which she had never seen from her Los Angeles apartment.

Llamas and children make a special combination. An inability to carry much weight often limits children to short stays in the backcountry. The docile, moderately sized llama provides the perfect answer by carrying the load for the youngsters. Every year we lead a trip for kids ages nine to eleven. Two adult leaders accompany eight children and as many llamas. Each child leads and cares for a llama throughout the trip. Many returning children want to lead the same llama year after year. Children under eighty pounds can ride on the back of a llama

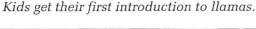

Kids get their first introduction to llamas.

12

outfitted with a small pony saddle. An adult usually leads the llama that is carrying the child.

Sheep ranchers throughout the western United States and Canada are finding that llamas diligently protect lambs from domestic dogs and coyotes. Livestock owners report astounding results once they add a llama to their flock of sheep. Although llamas will accept and ignore the family dog in the pasture, they react very aggressively toward unfamiliar dogs and will drive them out of a field or patrol a fence line so that the dog cannot enter. One farm near ours regularly lost fifty percent of their lambs to domestic dogs. The owners were ready to give up the sheep business because of these losses. After they put a guard llama in with their flock their losses from dogs dropped to zero and have remained there for the past three years. Although a pack of dogs can attack and kill a llama, the threat of a strike from the front legs of a llama will discourage a single dog.

The llama's popularity has increased dramatically as more people have discovered them. Llamas assist in programs for the handicapped and serve as 4-H projects; they visit local nursing homes, march in parades, help raise funds for social and political causes, deliver balloon

Although llamas chase unknown dogs out of the pasture, they get along with the family dog.

bouquets, and accompany long-distance cross-country runners as they train. Some people have taught llamas to pull pony carts, and a group of graduate engineering students from University of Colorado specially designed a llama-drawn wheelchair/trail cart, called a Llama-ghini, that enables handicapped people to travel in the backcountry. Last winter, Amy's sister Naomi trained Cappy, one of our calmest llamas, to pull her fourteen-month-old daughter around on a sled. Although Naomi had no previous experience with llamas, the entire training took a matter of minutes.

Llamas seem to carry some kind of magic. The first time we brought a llama to visit a nursing home proved more nerve-racking for us than it did for Black-Eyed-Jack, our public relations llama. While we were worrying about how Jack would react to a strange building, Jack had climbed the front stairs of the nursing home and was on his way to the door. Once inside, Jack took his time to meet and greet each person, putting his nose in each resident's face and sniffing. The folks were ecstatic about having a llama in their living room. They each had a story to tell about animals in their past, and Jack had sparked twinkles in many eyes.

Driving with llamas. Black-eyed Jack quickly learned to pull a cart.

14

– 2 –

TRAITS, GAITS, and LLAMA BASICS

The Perfect Pack Animal?

The llama makes a superb pack animal. A unique foot design, efficient gait and metabolism, special blood structure, and calm personality are just a few of their attributes. In a discussion of the wonderful traits of the llama, the foot seems like the logical place to start. In the same way a house will crumble without a proper foundation, a pack animal is only as good as his feet. The feet are the connection between the animal and the earth over which it travels.

As the llama evolved over millions of years it did not follow the well-established trend of foot development. Other ungulates or hoofed animals, such as the deer and horse, developed from digitigrade (walking on toes like a cat or dog) to unguligrade (walking on the tips of the toes). By walking on the tips of their toes, ungulates extended the length of their legs. This allowed them a longer, more efficient stride and more speed to escape predators.

The camelid, however, went from digitigrade to nearly unguligrade and then back to digitigrade. This deviation from the standard course of foot development evidently provided better support on soft substrates and compensated for the instability associated with the pacing gait (more on this later). Whatever the reason, the result was a padded, digitigrade foot placing a large surface area in contact with the earth.

This large, wide foot provided stability and exceptional surefootedness for the llama. To the novice looking at the llama's foot, however, many of these secrets are hidden. When I first saw a llama's foot, I thought it was a split hoof like that of a deer, goat, or sheep. Only when I lifted the foot and observed the underside, did I see that it was not at all cloven, but webbed. The soft, rounded, leather pad that makes up the bottom of the foot extends under two toenails. The toenails provide traction in the snow and mud, while the wide, soft leather pad offers stability and a light tread on fragile backcountry environments.

The common gait for a llama is the pace, a type of locomotion where the feet on the same side of the body move forward at the same time

15

A llama's foot. Note the soft pad and well-trimmed toenail.

Scent glands on inside and outside of llama's rear legs.

in a two-beat rhythm. In contrast, the normal gait for a horse or dog is the walk, where the front and hind feet move in an alternate four-beat rhythm. The pace allows the llama to cover more distance with less energy than it would walking. The sparse vegetation in the Andes Mountains probably sparked the development of the pacing gait because the llama needed to cover great distances to find sufficient food.

You might be asking yourself, if the pace is so efficient, then why didn't the horse and the dog develop this gait also? The answer is lateral instability. With both feet on one side of the body moving at the same time, the animal has less side-to-side stability and can more easily fall over sideways. The llama, however, has been able to compensate for this with its large foot and with special ligaments in the fetlock.

In addition to the normal pace, a llama can also walk, trot, gallop, and bounce. The llama walks only occasionally, when going up a steep hill. The trot, though rarely used, serves as an intermediate step to get from the pace to the gallop. The bounce resembles the movement of a western mule deer—all four feet contact and leave the ground at about the same time. Llamas usually bounce just before dark in a playful display of excess energy. It is a sight to see an entire herd of llamas bouncing in single file about the pasture.

We first encountered bouncing llamas one crisp spring evening just after sunset, a rosy glow still in the sky. Our female llamas and their young were running about the pasture. Then we noticed one of the babies bouncing off all four feet at one time. Within minutes, the llamas—older moms and all—were bouncing, their wool fluffing out around them. The evening glow combined with the llamas' fluffy wool made it look like the llamas were floating! The show lasted only a few minutes before the llamas calmed to a walk. We now make a point of being visiting the pasture just before dark in hopes of catching another bouncing llama show.

The sparse vegetation that influenced the development of the llama's specialized foot and paced gait also affected the llama's metabolism. In order to survive on scarce rations, the llama learned to metabolize very efficiently. A ruminant like goats, sheep, and cattle, the llama regurgitates a cud from one of its three stomachs and then chews the food a second time. Unlike

Sequoia and Hannibal enjoy snacking on the trail when the pack string takes a break.

goats, sheep, and cattle, llamas have a more continuously active fore-stomach and more frequent cycles of rumination than other livestock. This, combined with special digestive enzymes and the ability to recycle urea, allows llamas to thrive on low-protein foods such as the pine needles, sedges, and shrubs they nibble along the trail. Consequently, little if any of the pack llama's load needs to be llama food. Other less efficient pack stock must graze in lush meadows or carry large quantities of hay or grain to feed themselves.

Another unique characteristic of the llama is its blood. Llamas evolved grazing at elevations between 12,000 and 17,000 feet above sea level on the altiplano, a high flat plain in Peru and Bolivia. At these elevations oxygen is scarce, but the llama has developed a unique blood structure that can cope with the oxygen deficiency. The animal's hemoglobin has a much greater affinity to absorb oxygen than does that of other mammals. The blood also contains more red corpuscles. This unusual blood structure allows the llama to function efficiently as a pack animal even at high elevations. Llamas can go from sea level to 15,000 feet without needing time to adjust to the altitude.

We wished we had llama blood when we traveled by train across the dusty Bolivian altiplano—altitude sickness is not fun. The llamas we passed obviously were having no problems with the thin air; they frolicked happily as we passed in the train. Although llamas do well at very high elevations, they can also live at lower elevations. People all over the United States and Canada are raising llamas at low elevations, even at sea level.

Curious and social by nature, free-roaming llamas stick close to camp (within ¼ mile).

18

Personality: Spitting is a Bad Rap

Intelligent, companionable, gentle, curious, and calm are all words that describe llamas. With hidden surprises along the trail to interrupt your pack trip—packs slipping off, grouse flushing underfoot, a chance meeting with a bear—these are invaluable characteristics for pack stock. When facing the unexpected, rest assured your llama will remain relatively composed.

One spring three local children were eager to help us with our pre-season llama conditioning, so we all headed for the foothills behind our house, the three children and their llamas leading the way. Little did we know that our neighbor chose that day to announce the coming of spring—by firing a round (of blanks, thank goodness) from his authentic Civil War cannon. When the blast went off, we were standing only sixty yards from the muzzle of the cannon. Two of the llamas stepped sideways, then eyed the cannon through the trees. The third llama never jumped at all; instead, he watched Jessica, age six and the youngest of the three children, run circles around him as she cried hysterically.

With their calm disposition and moderate size, llamas are safe animals. They do not bite and rarely kick. The one full-force kick either of us has received produced only a light bruise. The fact that you are on the ground and not riding high on the animal's back probably contributes most to safety. People with no previous experience with stock feel safe leading a llama after just a few minutes of training.

While on the trail, you need not worry that your llama will run away. Llamas have a strong herd instinct, and most will go to great lengths to stay among other llamas. Because of this, we discourage isolating a single llama from the others. They are such social creatures that a llama that has been out of the pasture for only a few hours will return to a hero's welcome from his pasture-mates. On the trail, this strong social drive works in your favor. Even the laziest llama will strive to keep up with his more energetic companions. In camp, the llama allowed to graze freely will stay nearby if he has bonded to the other confined llamas. Occasionally, we encounter an independent llama that enjoys staying by himself. But the bottom line for the llama owner is that, unless yours is an independent animal, you should own at least two llamas.

Kids and llamas create a special combination. Black-eyed Jack is a great companion for Ira, who wasn't at all sure he wanted to come on this hike. By the end of the day, Jack had completely won Ira over.

When we display our llamas at the fair each summer, people frequently ask "Do they spit?" Our best response is to compare spitting llamas with biting dogs. Yes, llamas may spit and dogs may bite, but neither does so very often. Generally, llamas spit at each other during arguments over pecking order or food. An extremely irate llama will lay its ears back in warning long before spitting. The foul smell of the cud is just as obnoxious for the spitter as the spitee. Therefore llamas spit only as a last resort. You can tell when two llamas have had a disagreement—they both walk around with their mouths open, trying to get rid of the terrible odor.

Llama Senses

We don't know exactly how one would measure intelligence in a llama, but if ease of training indicates intelligence, they are certainly very smart creatures. A six-month-old llama can learn to wear a halter and be led in about three fifteen-minute sessions. A two- or three-year-old llama who has learned to lead can also learn to pack in about three fifteen-minute sessions.

Sharp perception and a built-in alarm call make llamas excellent night patrollers. When the llama sees, hears, or smells danger, he often sounds an alarm-call loud enough to wake the most sound sleeper. The call sounds half-way between a donkey braying and a person laughing.

One evening we were hiking with Black-Eyed-Jack, a four-year-old pack llama. Jack suddenly froze and stared at a clump of bushes 100 yards up the hill. His large brown eyes and banana-shaped ears focused sharply on the seemingly innocuous bushes. Periodically, he rotated one of his ears to listen for sounds from the trail behind us but then quickly refocused on the bushes. We looked into the bushes but saw nothing. Still Jack would not budge. Finally, we got Jack to start moving. Four steps later, two white-tailed deer bounded from the bushes. As we continued along the trail Jack let out an "I-told-you-so" hum. The keen senses of a llama can be equally helpful for the animal-seeking naturalist, photographer, or bow hunter—or for impressing your hiking friends with your woodsmanship.

Llamas also offer much for the person seeking companionship—the human-llama kind. One can take either of two attitudes about packing with llamas. One approach would be to consider your pack llama just another piece of equipment. As long as you take care of your equipment, your llama will pack supplies in and out of the backcountry. But we would strongly advise against this philosophy. You would be short-changing yourself. We find it more fulfilling to think of our llamas as companions, all of us setting out on a journey together. Without our companion, we would be carrying all the gear. Without us, our llama would be stuck in the barn eating hay rather than enjoying a smorgasbord of delightful tastes, sights, and sounds on the trail. A llama makes a very good companion indeed.

Woolly and Willing

Although llamas seem almost custom designed for packing, some of you may be concerned about the environmental degradation livestock cause. After all, a llama is a pack animal and the two of you will damage the environment more than if you simply packed supplies on your back. You are right. We all must decide whether to use pack stock or to pack supplies on your back. But before making that decision, you need to know just how much damage a llama will cause and how that impact compares to hiker and horse use.

We would like to be able to quote studies that quantitatively measure the impact of llamas on different backcountry environments, but no such studies exist. Based on the research that has been done, most agree that a llama causes more damage than a backpacker and less than a horse. Horses have considerably more impact on trails than hikers. Based on our observations, the impact of the llama falls much closer to that of the hiker than the horse. Comments such as "a llama has as little impact as a white-tailed deer" and "llamas have significantly less impact on trails than horses" were common in the research conducted by the U.S. Forest Service and the U.S. Park Service. (See Appendix for references.)

While bow-hunting one fall, we have compared llama tracks to elk tracks. A small herd of five elk had recently used the section of trail we were hiking. Curious about the similarity of the tracks, I tied my llama and walked back down the trail for a comparison. The llama's tracks were difficult to distinguish from the elk's tracks, even though the llama's foot is not cloven as the elk's. The leather pad on the llama is continuous across the foot, but it creases in the center—making a track that appears cloven. The only difference was a slightly larger gap between the pads in the llama track.

More interesting was the difference in disturbed soil. The llama actually disturbed the soil less than the walking elk. Farther back on

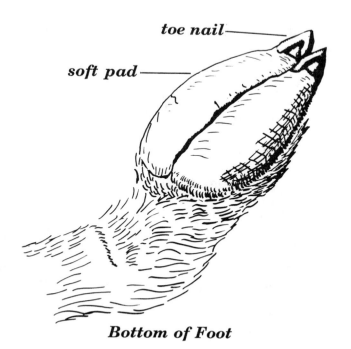

toe nail

soft pad

Bottom of Foot

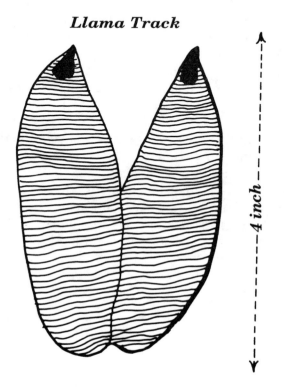

Llama Track

4 inch

the trail, I observed where both the llama and the elk had walked through a muddy section of the trail. In the mud the llama's track looked more rounded and less like an elk track. The leather part of the pad that had formed the crease on the hard surface was now helping support the llama in the mud. The llama's foot sank less into the mud than the elk's.

The bottom of the llama's foot is a soft, round, leather pad. The horse hoof, by comparison, is a hard structure, the very rigidity of which probably accounts for much of its trail destruction. A hardened hoof does not conform to small abnormalities in the trail—sticks are crushed or upended, small rocks are rolled out of their beds. To make matters worse, most horses are shod before going into the backcountry. The steel horseshoe has the same effect on the soil as a biscuit cutter does on dough. In contrast, the padded llama foot will mold and conform to the trail surface.

To determine the effects of stock on a campsite one must consider not only the foot, but also the metabolism and the size of the animal. Llamas and most large animals, including horses and mules, will consume 2% of their body weight in dry food matter daily. A 1,000 pound horse will consume 20 pounds of feed per day. Even the heaviest pack llama, weighing 400 to 450 pounds, will eat less than half that amount—eight pounds per day. After examining the browsing habits of llamas, personnel at Sequoia-Kings Canyon National Park in California determined that llamas have approximately one-third the overall impact of other pack stock.

Livestock can seriously degrade a campsite by trampling an area when they are confined. Picketing causes the most damage because the animal repeatedly tramples the same area. Temporary corrals are better, but the corralled stock still trample a relatively small area. The best method for managing stock in camp is to let them roam freely. Pack-stock that are allowed to roam freely will spread their impact in less concentrated doses over a larger area.

Llamas are very social creatures and most will do anything to stay with their woolly companions. If you confine one of the llamas, the rest can be left free to roam—allowing you to keep an eye on them but greatly reducing the amount of trampling.

We are convinced that llamas physically have little impact on the backcountry. But how do they fit socially? How do other users relate to the stock? Seeing the feces of domesticated animals while in the backcountry may lessen the wilderness experience for some hikers. Livestock also help spread non-native plants by dispersing seeds in their feces and in the hay carried in for pack stock to eat.

However, only an elk scat expert can distinguish the small pile of cylindrical llama pellets from those of an elk. The trail is not full of flies swarming about the llama's small pile either, since the llama will most often get off the trail to do its business. Further, the llama's efficient metabolism allows them to visit the backcountry without the need of supplemental hay for feed, and their digestive process destroys most seeds that they do ingest.

The llamas' charm and uniqueness certainly contribute to their acceptance in the backcountry. Rangers using llamas at Mt. Rainier National Park cited public acceptance of llamas as one of their most attractive features. The llama actually helped facilitate communication between the rangers and the public. Also, people with no experience with pack stock feel comfortable around the moderately sized animal. We have received overwhelmingly positive responses from hikers we have encountered along the trail.

The decision whether to use pack stock and what type of pack stock is a choice for each person. Certain fragile environments will tolerate no pack stock use whatsoever. In those areas you should carry supplies on your back. It is our belief and experience, however, that most environmentally responsible hikers can feel comfortable using llamas in most backcountry settings.

Buddies. Llamas are very social creatures and should always have a companion animal (llama or other species).

Llama Limitations

Thus far in this chapter we have only discussed the positive aspects of the llama as a pack animal. Although llamas are extremely well suited for packing, they do have limitations and a few unfavorable characteristics. As we discuss the limitations of the llama, please keep in mind that the positive factors far outweigh the negative.

Most owners deem undesirable the llama's distant, unaffectionate attitude. If you are looking for a pet that will come running to you to be scratched on the back or hugged, you had better forget the llama. Llamas in the pasture respect each other's personal space and keep their distance from each other. With very few exceptions, llamas do not liked being touched, much less fondled by humans. Llamas appear to merely tolerate affection. A llama owner can easily accept this minor drawback by learning to enjoy them from a respectable distance. You only need to realize that most llamas like their space and that it is nothing personal.

Another concern of new llama owners is finding a veterinarian with experience treating llamas. Llamas are less plentiful in North America than other livestock, so your local livestock vet may have limited experience with them. Fortunately a llama's ailments are very similar to those of more common domestic animals such as sheep, goats, and cows. Further, llamas are hardy animals that require remarkably little medical attention.

The llama's limited weight-carrying capacity presents perhaps the most obvious limitation. While a horse or mule can carry 200 pounds, a llama can pack only 80 to 100 pounds. Most loads are carried in panniers—one on the left and one on the right. This means that a llama cannot carry any single object greater than 50 pounds because the weight in one pannier must be balanced by equal weight in the other pannier. The hind quarter of an elk, for instance, weighs about 100 pounds with the bone in. Since you could not put the entire 100-pound hindquarter on one side of the llama, you would need to bone out the meat and divide it in two before packing it out.

Each llama has its own weight limit. Do not make the mistake of overloading your llama or you will see a demonstration of the original "sit-in." For all the positive aspects of their personality, llamas can be very stubborn if overloaded. An overburdened llama will lie down in the trail and nothing short of a bulldozer can move him.

– 3 –

CARE AND FEEDING

Once you decide you want a pack llama, you need to plan how you will properly house, pasture, fence, and feed him so that he stays healthy and happy at home. Before rushing out to purchase your first llama, consider the time commitment involved in owning an animal. You are committing yourself to a daily routine of caring for your llama. Whenever you plan to go away, someone else must come check on your llama. You can leave several days' worth of hay at a time, but it is still a good idea to check on the llama at least once a day.

You must also consider the financial commitment and be able to meet your llama's basic needs: good hay, access to water, shelter, and routine vaccinations and worming. Owners typically spend less than $200 per year to feed and care for a llama, but you cannot compromise on these basic expenditures. Your llama depends on you; his well-being is entirely your responsibility. These commitments should not be taken lightly.

A Simple Home

One reason llamas are relatively inexpensive animals to keep is their simple housing requirements. Llamas need only a simple shelter to protect them from extreme hot and cold and wind. If you have several male pack llamas, and no female llamas, then your llamas should be able to share feeders, shelter, and pasture space. This will help to keep your costs down.

Llamas have survived the rugged winters of the Andes Mountains for centuries, and can withstand temperatures well below zero. As long as they have a snug place to get out of the wind during the winter, they will be fine. A three-sided shelter, oriented to provide protection from the worst winter storms is adequate for your pack llamas. Bedding such as straw will provide good insulation for your llamas if you live in northern climates.

In general, llamas do best when they can come and go freely from their shelter, rather than being closed inside. Many winter mornings we go out to the barn to find several inches of fresh snow piled on the back of a llama who has chosen to sleep out. Their wool insulates them, preventing their body heat from escaping and melting the snow.

Just as their wool protects llamas from the winter cold, it also insulates them from the summer heat. However, in extreme heat and humidity, your llamas will suffer. In fact, extreme summer heat will affect your llamas more than cold winter weather. During the summer, llamas need shade. If you live in an area with hot, humid summers, you will need to provide a means for your llamas to cool off. You should also shear your llamas if their wool becomes too thick or matted to allow adequate air circulation. People in the southern United States have found ingenious methods to keep their llamas cool in the summer: providing children's wading pools for their llamas to lie in, installing sprinkler systems in the pasture, using sprinklers to cool a metal barn roof plus running fans inside to circulate the cool air, and a placing a layer of cool damp sand (which can be sprayed daily) on the barn floor.

If you live in a warm climate, your llamas will become somewhat acclimated to the heat, however, every llama owner should be familiar with and watch for signs of heat stress.

Housing: Llamas require minimal shelter. This old barn provides ample protection for Aquila—windbreak in winter and shade in the summer.

Heat stress can be fatal if not treated quickly. See First Aid (chapter ten) for more information on heat exhaustion and symptoms and treatment of heat stress.

You must also consider where you could put a sick llama in an emergency. If your vet has overnight facilities this may not be a concern. Otherwise, if you do not have a barn, you should think of possibilities, such as a garage or shop that could be temporarily converted to keep an animal warm. You will probably never need to use such an area, but it is wise to be prepared.

We once brought Annie, a baby llama orphaned at one day old, into our basement wood room to keep her warm and convenient for frequent feedings. For her first week, she spent her nights in the wood room and her days outside with the herd, and soon became strong enough to stay outside all the time. At six weeks old, we grafted her onto a mama llama who accepted Annie as her own.

Besides providing shelter for your llamas, you will need to shelter your stored hay. Try to purchase your winter's supply of hay and store it under cover conveniently near your feeding area. Once you estimate the number of bales you will need, you may be surprised to find that you can store several months' worth of hay in a small storage shed. Depending upon the amount of rain and snow in your area, you may be able to store your hay outside under a plastic tarp. However, outside storage will mean more wasted hay since moisture will cause the hay to turn moldy. An alternative might be to buy your hay from someone who will allow you to pick it up a few bales at a time.

Pasturing

Llamas evolved as a free-ranging species, foraging as they traveled. Turning your llamas out into pasture is as important for their mental health as for their physical health. During the summer you can easily sustain three llamas on one acre of prime, irrigated pasture without supplemental feeding. If you have wooded or less productive land, you should account for that in figuring how many animals you can keep or plan on feeding supplemental hay year-round. Llamas love to explore large, wooded hillsides, eating bark, leaves, and weeds. In fact, our llamas prefer exploring a 40-acre wooded hillside and would choose it any day over feasting in a flat, lush, three-acre hayfield.

When planning your pasture, remember that llamas are browsers (like deer) and will eat leaves and weeds along with grass. They prefer a variety and do not need the high protein of legumes. Given a choice, your llama will usually eat only those plants that are good for him. Therefore, unless your llama is seriously underfed, he will steer away from poisonous plants. See First Aid (chapter ten) and Appendix for additional information and references on poisonous plants.

Be wary of a pasture with a large amount of alfalfa. Fresh alfalfa can cause bloating in ruminants, such as cows and llamas, due to a chemical reaction in their stomachs. A llama suffering from bloat will have a swollen belly, and because the swollen belly will press against his lungs, he will have difficulty breathing. You will hear a small grunt as he exhales each breath. He will be uncomfort-

Our llamas prefer the 40-acre wooded hillside over the flat, lush field for pasture.

able. Without immediate veterinary treatment, bloating can kill an animal. Contact your vet immediately if you suspect bloat.

Ticks, which carry many diseases, are another concern in selecting pasture for llamas. Even normal, healthy ticks can cause tick paralysis. They live in brushy areas, so during tick season, you should avoid putting your llamas into a pasture with a lot of underbrush. Tick season can last almost year-round in warmer climates, or only a few spring months in colder regions. Some areas have a fall tick season as well. For more information about ticks and preventive measures you can take, see First Aid (chapter ten).

Fences

Three types of fencing are available commercially: wooden, electric, and wire. All three will work well to confine the happy llama. Wooden fences work very well for llamas and are, without question, the most attractive. Unfortunately wooden fencing is also the most expensive. Electric fencing is a good alternative because it is safe, less expensive, and easy to move. Llamas seem to remember getting shocked and respect even the unplugged electric fence. Also, electric fences are a good way to discourage neighborhood dogs that could crawl under a wooden fence. Baby llamas are particularly vulnerable to attacks by dogs. Another way to make a dog-proof fence is with woven wire, also called field fencing or sheep fencing. Llamas will stay inside woven wire fences, especially if there is a wooden top rail or top electric wire. If barbed wire is already in place, it will work. However, a barbed wire fence presents tremendous danger of injury should a llama try to jump it. Therefore, we strongly discourage installing new barbed wire.

Depending upon your needs and size of your property, you can use a combination of types of fencing. Be sure to make the fence that runs along the perimeter of your property the most secure. We have found that wire field fencing with wooden posts and top bars meets our needs for perimeter fencing. It has the advantage of keeping young llamas in and dogs out. Depending upon your needs, you can then subdivide your pastures with moveable electric or permanent wooden fences.

When planning your fences, remember that llamas usually will not challenge a fence. However, if they feel threatened or are chased, they can jump a five- or six-foot fence. Therefore, it is best if you have a smaller, more

secure area available to use when catching your llamas. You might also use such an area when you first bring your llama home.

Ideally your llama should get acquainted with your other llamas across the fence before you turn the newcomer out to pasture with your other llamas. Certainly you should avoid turning a new llama out into a pasture with an electric fence if he has not yet learned about electric fences. Llamas are basically homebodies: once they have settled in for a few days, they will want to stay at home with their

Woven-wire field fencing with a wooden top rail has the advantage of keeping dogs out of the pasture.

llama buddies and will be less likely to challenge your perimeter fence.

In laying out your pastures, think about ease of movement before deciding where to put gates. Animals in each pasture will need to have access to water, food, and shelter, and you will need to move easily through the pastures to feed and water your llamas without having to wrestle open large, unwieldy gates. So, you will want small walk-through gates. You also may want to drive farm machinery through your pastures to mow them or deliver hay. Therefore, you will want additional gates at least twelve feet wide into every pasture.

Besides considering your convenience in moving around your property, you will want to plan your pastures so you can easily herd your llamas from one pasture to another, to the barn, or into smaller paddocks or catch pens.

Many people have laid out their fields and paddocks so that the barn and hay storage area are at the center, and each pen or series of pens extends out from the barn. The barn itself is subdivided, with hay and water in each of the separate pens inside the barn. Although this centralized layout greatly simplifies feeding and watering chores, its shortcomings become evident if you have two males who fight across the fence and need to be separated or if you want to quarantine an animal. In these situations you will need a completely separate area where llamas cannot fight across a fence or touch noses.

The Low-Protein Diet

As modified ruminant herbivores, llamas digest plant material in a unique, three-compartment stomach. Llamas evolved an exceptionally efficient metabolism from consuming low protein feeds in the high regions of the Andes Mountains of South America. This means that they get more energy from their food than most other livestock species. Llamas are up to 50 percent more efficient in metabolizing their food than horses or sheep. Their small size (350 pounds average) also means that they do not require much food. Surprisingly, the efficiency of a llama's metabolism increases as the quality of the feed decreases.

An average quality grass hay (10 to 12 percent protein) will likely meet your llama's nutritional needs. However, you can choose from various feeding options, including oat hay, alfalfa hay, grain, a commercially prepared complete ration, or pasture.

Before purchasing hay, seek the advice of a knowledgeable person, such as your local county Extension Agent (a service of the U. S. Department of Agriculture). Your Extension office will also provide useful publications from the U. S. Department of Agriculture.

In selecting hay, check the color, stem thickness, moisture content, and smell. A pure green color identifies a hay with maximum vitamin content. Avoid large, thick stems as the llamas will find these unpalatable, leaving you with considerably more wasted hay. Excessive moisture will cause mold later on. Hay should smell fresh and not musty. Dusty hay can cause respiratory problems, but if you must feed it, you can sprinkle the flakes with water or shake out the dusty flakes completely before offering it to the llamas outdoors.

Allow hay to cure at least three weeks before you begin using it. If it is too damp when it is baled, it will begin to mold within three weeks after baling. If you are buying your hay out of the field, you might check with the farmer and see if you can return the hay if it should turn moldy. Of course, the best judges of the hay are the llamas themselves: buy several bales and let your llamas sample it before purchasing a large amount. What you feed your llamas will affect their ability to perform as pack llamas, so do not scrimp on the quality of your hay.

Your llamas' feeder should always contain some average quality grass hay (this is called free-choice feeding), but you should limit the amount of fresh hay to be sure the animals consume the less desirable stems and stalks. Most other livestock are fed several flakes of hay at a time and consume the entire amount within a matter of hours. Free-choice feeding of llamas simulates natural grazing and browsing patterns. The llamas eat several times during the day, chewing their cud between meals. Feeding free choice also removes the need for a specific mealtime, allowing more flexibility in the llama owner's schedule.

A llama will consume approximately two percent of his body weight in dry food matter daily. This means that an average pack llama weighing 350 pounds will eat up to seven pounds of hay per day. If you feed hay 365 days a year, with no supplemental pasture, your llama will consume approximately 2,555 pounds (one and a quarter tons) of hay in one year. With about 32 bales per ton of hay, your llama will eat about 40 bales of hay in a year. Some of the hay will be wasted around the feeder, so your llama will actually go through one and one-half tons or 50 bales of hay per year.

Pasturing your llama during the summer will decrease his annual hay consumption to less than one ton. Pasture in the spring and early summer, when the plants are actively growing, will have a higher protein content, possibly eliminating the need for any supplemental hay during those months. Expect to pay considerably less for hay during the summer, and up to twice as much by late spring when supplies are limited. We pay between $50 and $75 for a ton of hay in the fall, less if we pick it up out of the field. Your annual expenditures for hay will vary depending upon your locality and the availability and type of hay.

Each llama's energy requirements must be considered in designing your feeding program. Young, growing animals will need more protein than mature animals. Depending upon the quality of the hay you are feeding, you may need to supplement your immature llamas with corn or other grains. Adult males require more food when they are packing (25 percent increase for light activity, 50 percent for heavy work) than when they are at home in the pasture. Extremely cold weather also places higher demands on the llamas, and we advise that you increase the calorie content in their diet, sometimes by as much as 50 percent. Because your llama can consume only so much hay each day, simply feeding more hay may not meet his daily energy requirements. You may elect to add high-energy concentrates (such as flaked corn), vegetable oils (such as corn oil), or whole cottonseed to his diet. Any changes in feed, even the introduction of a higher protein hay (such as alfalfa hay), must be made gradually so your llama can adjust.

When your llama is out on the trail he will not have time to eat hay or graze as he would at home. Although he will forage some at night, this will not meet his energy requirements for heavy activity. You should plan to bring along a high-energy supplemental feed, such as flaked corn, or a commercially prepared ration. You can also add high-calorie corn oil, soy bean meal, or whole cottonseed to his feed. Try out a small amount of the feed

Llamas enjoy sampling from the smorgasboard along the trail. When trekking, you will need to pack only one to two pounds of supplemental feed per day for your llama.

at home to be sure your llama will like it. We find that flaked corn mixed with alfalfa pellets, plus some evening grazing, meets the energy requirements of our pack males when they are out on the trail. While on a llama trek, we feed one to two pounds of this mixture per day to each llama, depending upon the level of activity. We feed half of this amount in the morning and half in the evening. Be aware that your llama will need to consume more water when eating these dry feeds out on the trail.

In addition to the high-protein concentrate feed, llamas require at least 25 percent roughage for their digestive system to function properly. Including roughage (such as alfalfa pellets) in the ration you are feeding and allowing your llamas to get some roughage by grazing while they are on the trail will ensure that they get the roughage they need.

The balance between calcium and phosphorous, as well as the inclusion of copper, zinc, selenium, and many other minerals in the diet, plays as big a role in your llama's overall health as the protein content of the feed. Grains and corn are typically high in phosphorous, while alfalfa hay is high in calcium. Llamas generally cannot get enough salt from the solid salt blocks, so provide a free choice mix of loose salt and minerals as a convenient dietary supplement. Depending upon where you live, your llama may require other supplemental minerals. Your vet and other local llama owners can help you design a feeding program that will supply necessary minerals, vitamins, and protein for your llama.

When designing a feeding plan, consider cost, local availability and nutritional balance. We have found that a diet of straight grass hay, fed free choice, works well for our pack llamas year-round. In the summer, they graze in the pasture but still like to eat a little hay. We only supplement their diet when they are on the trail. By eating grass hay, rather than alfalfa hay, our llamas do not grow fat over the winter. Most llama owners in North America tend to overfeed their llamas. An overweight llama will overheat in hot weather or when he is under stress, such as on a pack trip. Your llama will be healthier and happier if he is in good condition, rather than overfed.

One Good Drink a Day

At home, fresh clean water should always be available to your llama. Your llama's daily water needs will vary from 5 to 10 percent of his body weight, depending upon his level of activity, air temperature, and moisture content of the feed. A llama that grazes on fresh green grasses may not need any supplemental water at all, whereas a llama that eats only dry hay will need several gallons of water a day. A 350-pound llama will usually drink two to three gallons of water a day, but can consume up to five gallons of water on an extremely hot day. On the trail, one good drink a day will usually suffice, although two drinks is better.

A Healthy Llama

Many articles and several books (see Appendix) on the market provide comprehensive information on almost every aspect of health care for llamas. In this section, we introduce the tools and knowledge you will need to provide the routine health care your pack llama will need and to know when to seek the advice and care of your veterinarian.

Vaccinations and Worming

Your llama will need to be vaccinated with a multiple vaccine that includes tetanus, and be wormed several times a year. Consult your local veterinarian to set up a vaccination and worming schedule for your llamas.

If you live in a warm climate you will need to give worming medicine more often than in colder climates. Cold weather (temperatures below freezing for several consecutive months) kills off some of the larvae. To check the effectiveness of the worming medicine, have your vet examine a fecal sample five days to two weeks after worming. The length of time between administering worming medicine and checking the fecal sample depends upon the type of medicine and type of worm. Varying the active worming ingredient throughout the year will increase its effectiveness.

After observing your veterinarian give shots and worming medicine, you may feel ready to administer the oral medicine and injections yourself. In many rural areas, where the vets travel considerable distances to farms, they encourage livestock owners to administer shots and worming medicines to their own animals. After receiving instructions from your vet, you will likely find it more convenient and less expensive to perform this routine health care yourself.

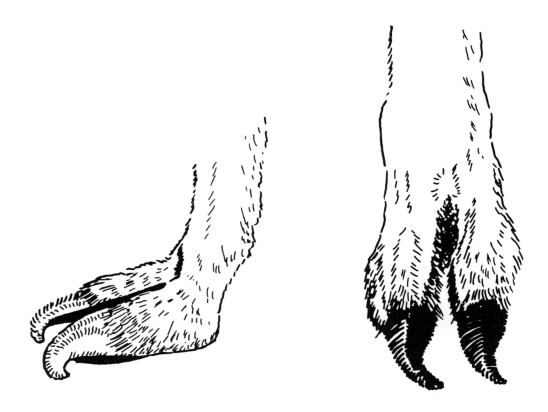

These toenails need trimming.

Toenails

Unless your pasture is extremely rocky, your llama's toenails will need trimming. The toenails should curve down until they are flush with the bottom of the foot. Once the toenail grows beyond the level of the pad, it should be trimmed. If allowed to grow unchecked, long toenails will force the llama to walk back on its heels, causing serious damage to the foot.

We once tried to work with a llama whose toenails had been neglected by his owners for such a long time that he stood completely rocked back on his heels. We trimmed his toenails until they appeared to be normal, then took him out on a short hike. The next day he looked like he was tip-toeing around the pasture. His feet were so sensitive from not touching the ground that it took all summer for his pads to toughen up. His owners no longer take him out on the trail, so he must be content to keep his llama buddies company in the pasture.

You should check your llama's toenails at least twice a year either by picking up his feet one at a time or by examining the nail while your llama stands on a hard flat surface, such as cement or pavement. Some llamas will need their nails trimmed four or five times a year; others wear them off constantly and never need trimming.

Trimming the toenails becomes fairly simple if the llama has been desensitized and trained to allow you to handle his feet. (See Training and Conditioning, chapter five, for more on desensitizing your llama.) If your

HOOF NAIL NIPPER

TOE SHEARS

HOOF PICK

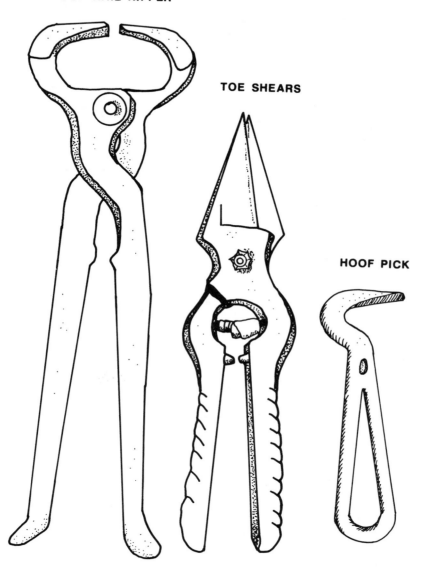

Toenail trimming tools. Use either the hoof nippers or the toe shears for trimming. The hoof pick is handy to remove manure or mud from the nail before trimming.

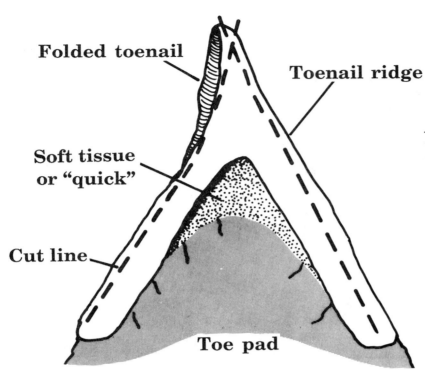

Folded toenail

Toenail ridge

Soft tissue or "quick"

Cut line

Toe pad

Trim the sides of the nails first as shown along the cut lines. Take care to avoid cutting into the soft tissue or "quick" area as it will cause bleeding and pain to your llama. A deep cut into the "quick" can lead to an infection and lameness. Treat cut into "quick" with 7% iodine and pressure to stop any bleeding.

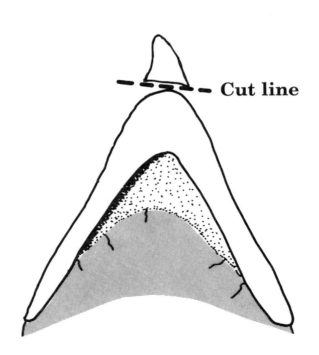

Cut line

Make your last cuts across the point of the nail.

36

llama will not allow you to pick up his feet, you may need to place him in some type of restraint chute. Trimming the toenails is much easier with two people: one to hold the foot and the other to trim. You can use a variety of clippers, including horse hoof nippers, horseshoe nail nippers (smaller), sheep hoof shears, or foot rot shears. Check with your local ranch or horseshoeing supply stores. Whatever type of clippers you select, be sure they have a sharp cutting edge. Shears should have rounded points so you will not jab the llama's leg.

To begin work on a foot, clean off the mud so that you can see the pad and nail. You can use a horse tool, called a hoof pick, to clean out the mud if necessary. If you are not sure, do not cut. A cut on a llama's pad is a serious injury that will keep him off the trail for the season. If your llama's toenails are severely overgrown, you may need to trim his nails gradually in several sessions. If your llama's nails have begun to twist, you may need to trim once a month for several months to straighten the nails.

Start clipping at the back edge of each nail and work toward the point, making several cuts. Then clip off the point, being careful not to cut the soft, fleshy center of the toenail. This area of the nail, called the quick, will bleed easily. If left alone, it will wear off by itself after the nail has been clipped away. Clip a little bit at a time, going back to snip more if needed.

If your llama has especially hard nails that do not wear down naturally, you can make an additional final cut along the ridgeline. This will eliminate some of the thickness and allow the nail to wear on its own. Be very cautious about making this cut as you do not want to make it so high or so deep to cause bleeding. Two smaller cuts are better than one big cut.

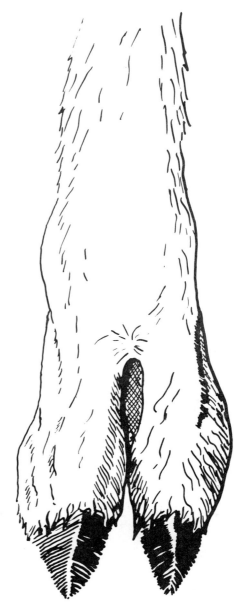

These nicely trimmed toenails are ready for the trail.

37

Removing Llama Fighting Teeth

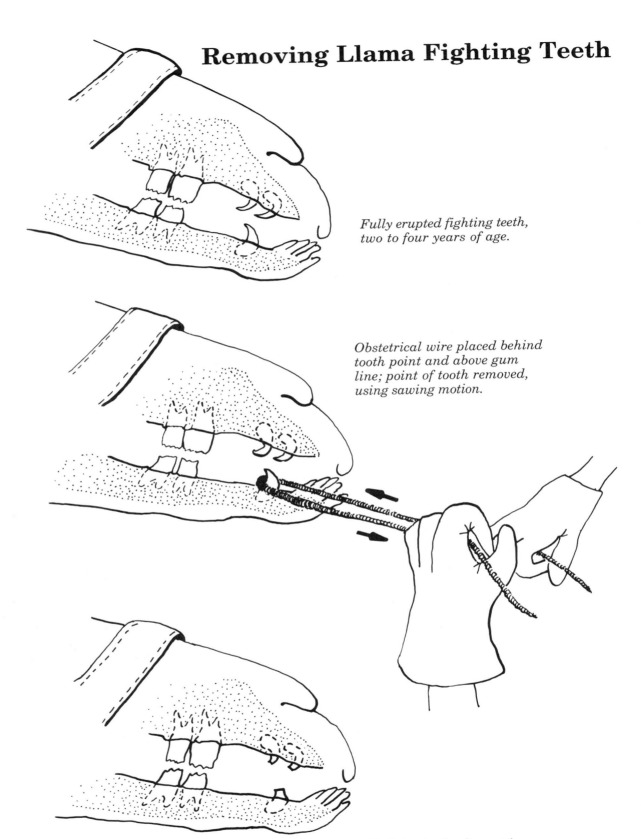

Fully erupted fighting teeth, two to four years of age.

Obstetrical wire placed behind tooth point and above gum line; point of tooth removed, using sawing motion.

Fighting teeth after cutting.

If your llama has a nail that curves, rather than grows straight, you can make a notch in the nail along the ridgeline. The notch will relieve some of the pressure that is causing the nail to twist, and will help straighten the nail over time.

Fighting Teeth

Adult male llamas who have not been gelded will grow fighting teeth in their upper and lower jaws. These sharp teeth angle backwards, making them dangerous weapons. Once a male is gelded and the teeth are removed, the teeth will not grow back. Males gelded young may never get them.

You or your veterinarian can easily remove fighting teeth by sawing with obstetrical wire. This sounds awful but is actually a quick and painless procedure. The center of the tooth is hollow and does not contain any nerve endings. The worst part for the llama is having someone's fingers in his mouth!

Tie your llama's head securely in a restraint chute so that he cannot move from side to side. One person is needed to hold the llama's lips apart while another person places

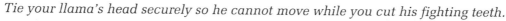
Tie your llama's head securely so he cannot move while you cut his fighting teeth.

Have a helper hold the llama's lips so you don't accidentally injure the llama with the wire.

the obstetrical wire around the top of the tooth and begins to gently draw the wire back and forth. You can use a one- to two-foot length of wire with handles on either end, or wrap the wire around your gloved fingers to keep it taut.

Both people should wear glasses or eye protection. After about five or six strokes the tooth will come flying out. Try to cut the tooth as close as possible to the gum line without cutting the gum. Be careful not to catch any part of the mouth, lips, or tongue in the sawing process. Check for fighting teeth once or twice a year in intact males, as they will grow back.

Records

Regardless of who administers vaccinations and worming medicine, trims toenails, or cuts fighting teeth, it is imperative to keep good records. Each llama should have his own folder with records of all his health care, including medications, injuries, and weight gain. These records are invaluable if your llama is injured and you need to know when he had his last tetanus shot, if you suspect illness and want to track his weight gain or loss, or if a potential buyer wants to know how often you have to trim your llama's toenails. Many people also include information such as miles traveled on pack trips, ribbons won at local fairs, and other events attended in each llama's records.

Recognizing Health Problems

As a llama owner, you can complete all the routine health care procedures. But when your llama starts acting strangely, it is time to call your vet. Veterinarians who have experience working with llamas are becoming more common, but do not wait until you have a problem before looking for a vet. A vet who has experience with other livestock such as goats, sheep, cows and horses, will be able to provide veterinary services for your llama. Ask other local llama owners for references to help you choose a vet, then help educate your vet by sharing publications and your own knowledge.

Since you see your llamas daily, you will be the best judge of the animals' health. Stoical by nature, llamas will not show discomfort until it is severe. Any changes in eating patterns, social interactions, or other behaviors could signal a problem. Abnormal behavior can be as subtle as standing off alone, standing with a humped back, or lying down frequently. Or it can be more obvious, such as labored breathing, lack of interest in feed, or a llama lying on his side. For more information about common symptoms of illness, particularly tick paralysis, see First Aid (chapter ten).

While knowing your llamas and their habits will help you protect your investment, you can also purchase mortality insurance. You will need a veterinarian's health certificate to apply for full mortality insurance for your llama. The cost for full mortality insurance is about 3.5 percent of the purchase price of the llama. You can also opt for the less expensive named perils insurance, which protects against death by fire, lightning, collapse of building, accidental shooting, attack by wild animals, and motor vehicle accident. Each company covers different perils, and the cost is about 1.25 percent of the purchase price of the llama. The Appendix lists names and addresses of livestock insurance companies that provide llama insurance.

Llamas are very social creatures and need a companion.

– 4 –

SELECTING YOUR
PACK LLAMA

One of your most important decisions will be selecting a llama. Purchasing a llama is an investment of time, money, and energy. However, the decision need not be difficult. Ninety percent of the work can and should be done before you even visit your first farm—it is called soul searching.

Ask yourself, and answer realistically, how often you will use the llama. Do you need the perfect pack llama, or will an average one do? Will you ever want to use your llama as a breeding stud? If so, you will not want to buy a gelding (a castrated male llama). Do you have the time and interest to train the llama yourself? If not, you will want to purchase an animal already trained to pack. Will you also use the llama for wool production? Spend time on these questions before you start to shop. Once you meet eyes with your first beautiful, cuddly llama, it will be difficult to remain objective.

You should also address the question of how many llamas to buy. Be aware that, because of their strong social nature, most llamas require the company of another llama for good mental health. A llama taken from a farm and isolated can become very lonely, even become sick. Most can get by if they have something or someone else to bond with. A goat or sheep makes an adequate companion for the llama. However, we recommend owning two llamas.

If you have never purchased or owned llamas, ask advice of others with more experience. A good way to get started is to visit other llama packers and ask them about their llamas. Which animal is their best packer? Why did they purchase him? Most llama packers are proud of their animals and enjoy sharing their expertise. Check with your local veterinarian or feed store, or at the county fair for names of local llama owners.

If no one in your area packs with llamas, visit a llama breeding operation at least to see the animals. Remember, however, these folks are in the business of producing llamas to look good and do not always understand what makes a good pack llama.

Even better than talking about it is to get firsthand packing experience before you start shopping. A number of commercial llama packers will pack you and your gear into the backcountry. This is an excellent, albeit somewhat costly, way to gain top-notch experience. A less expensive route is to rent llamas and do the trip yourself. The price of the rental often includes a pre-trip llama packing clinic. The more you learn before you buy, the better decision you will make. The Appendix lists llama organizations that can provide names of commercial packers in your area.

Gelding Versus Stud

Female llamas, because of their relatively high market value, are not normally used as packers. It is not worth exposing a valuable female llama to the risk of a broken leg or attack by wild animals. If the price of female llamas drops dramatically in the future, we expect to see females in the pack string. Until then, however, you have only two options: castrated males (called geldings) or intact males (called studs). Around the barn, studs will fight with each other to determine social rank. On the trail, however, studs fight much less and can work well together in a pack string. It really depends on the individual llama. One of my best packers is a stud. Some say studs are more energetic and less apt to lie down on the trail than geldings. Other llama packers think geldings are the only way to go because of their calm nature. We pack with both studs and geldings and see little difference in their willingness to work. If you have female llamas at home, as we do, you will probably want to keep the number of studs to a minimum to avoid the possibility of accidental breedings.

An Appropriate Age

Llamas reach full maturity somewhere between three and four years of age. Until then, putting a full load on your llama could injure him. Therefore, if you plan to pack with a llama the first season you own him, buy one at least three years old. If you can wait a season before fully loading him, buy a two-year-old and train him before he is fully grown. Two-year-olds can start to pack, but should not carry more than 20% of their body weight and never more than 40 pounds.

Llamas normally live fifteen to twenty years, but their packing life could be much shorter depending on how the llama is used, his health, conformation, and genetics, and environmental conditions. Many llama packers are finding that after ten years of heavy packing the llamas are ready to retire. Thus, a ten-year-old llama that has been packing since age three might not have many productive years left.

The Proper Build

It would be nice if we could just look at a llama to see if he would make a good pack animal. Unfortunately the personality of the llama plays a much greater role than looks in packing—and you cannot see personality. Unless the animal has a willing personality, the body type means nothing. Having said this, we will note that llama packers deem a certain body type most suitable for packing.

A llama-packing acquaintance explains the best body type with the phrase "football player versus basketball player." The football player body build is one of big muscles, husky and stout. In general, "football-player" llamas can carry heavy loads but become fatigued easily. The broad chest of the football player type causes excess side-to-side sway when the animal walks. Further, the rugged "football-player"

Orion, a regular in our pack string, has the "football player" type of build (left), while King is more of a "basketball player" type (right). Despite their different body builds, both are good packers.

types are shorter and have a shorter stride. The tall basketball player, however, will have long stringy muscles and greater endurance. A narrower chest with less associated sway and a longer stride allow a faster pace. The "basketball-player" type should make an excellent pack llama—if he has a good personality.

You can assess how large a young llama will grow by looking at his parents. Offspring from small llamas will themselves be smaller and capable of carrying less weight than a larger llama. Some llamas—noticeably smaller, woollier, and round-backed—retain close genetic ties to their cousins, the alpacas. Alpacas are bred for a specific purpose—to produce wool, not to carry loads. Alpacas have a distinctive rounded, sloping look to their hindquarters, and a tilted pelvis that does not bear weight well. When shopping for a pack animal, you will do well to avoid these small, woolly llamas, and instead select a flat-backed llama of average size.

McGruder has the large size, solid legs, and flat back that you should look for in a pack llama.

Personality

Assessing the body type of a llama becomes simple after a bit of practice. Determining a llama's personality, however, is much more difficult. In general, look for an inquisitive, not overly skittish animal that desires to please you. While it is difficult to recognize all elements in a llama's nature, two personality-types are easy to spot and should be avoided: the spitting llama and the over-friendly llama.

Llamas spit at one another as part of their normal behavior. Spitting is the llama's way of settling disputes. However, if a llama spits at you while you are haltering or working with him, you should not purchase this animal. Although there are ways of dealing with a spitting llama, this behavior may indicate a more serious personality problem, such as over-friendliness, that you would do well to avoid.

Beware the llama that runs to greet you and puts his nose in your face. Normal llamas shun attention from humans; an overly friendly male may suffer from berserk-male syndrome. Berserk-male syndrome often results from over-handling or bottle-feeding a baby male llama. The young llama bonds to the person holding the bottle—believing that person is its mother—and grows up thinking humans are llamas. When a male llama reaches maturity, he attempts to establish dominance over the rest of the herd—which in the case of the berserk male includes humans as well as llamas. The berserk male becomes extremely dangerous, often ramming, biting, or spitting at humans. Training and Conditioning (chapter 5) provides more information on how to prevent this problem among your own llamas.

Trained or Trainable?

While searching your soul earlier, you should have asked yourself if you wanted to purchase a trained-to-pack llama or an untrained llama. Training a llama to pack is fairly simple, involving ten to fifteen hours of work putting on the saddle and taking the animal on practice hikes. Of course, by purchasing an experienced pack llama you avoid the risk of buying a llama whose packing abilities are unknown. However, you can reduce your risk by taking the prospective llama on hikes prior to purchase.

In any case, learn to recognize the behaviors that indicate training. Ask the owner to describe the llama's level of training, then see if the llama's actions correspond with that report. If the owner struggles and grunts just to put a halter on, the llama is probably untrained or untrainable. The owner might view training as simply having the halter on once or twice, while you might think it means trained to pack.

But how can one tell if an untrained llama is trainable? The best way is to take it for a test walk. Most people would not buy a car without first test driving it. You should do no less with the llama. If the llama has met your other criteria, schedule a time to come back for a half-hour walk with him. Before going back to the farm, read chapter five, Training and Conditioning, to learn how to teach the llama some simple commands.

On the walk, try to teach the llama a simple exercise, such as walking under a low branch or jumping a fallen log. If the llama is reluctant, have him follow another llama through the obstacle, or back up to a simpler exercise. It may take several tries before the llama will follow you over a log or through brush. This half-hour walk should give you time to assess the llama's willingness to follow, the most important personality trait for a pack llama.

Wool

A llama's long wool is nice for spinning and makes the llama look cute and cuddly. However, long wool serves no purpose on a pack llama. The woollier your llama, the more difficult it is to brush out debris that gets embedded in the wool where the pack rides, causing extreme discomfort. Long wool also tends to catch in the pack's buckles and cinches, and llamas do not like having their wool pulled.

Llama wool has two components: coarse, outer guard hairs and finer under-wool. The guard hairs repel water and are less apt to attract seeds and twigs. It is possible to shear an exceptionally woolly llama and use him for packing. The guard hairs will grow back in several months, but the llama will be unable to shed

water in the meantime. If a recently shorn llama gets caught in a rainstorm, he will get soaked to the skin and severely chilled. For packing, then, it is best to buy a short-wool llama with many guard hairs.

The color of the llama does not affect the animal's ability to pack or its ability to control body heat. However, if you plan to use your llama on hunting trips, avoid solid dark colors so a hunter will not mistake your llama for a deer or elk. A white llama is the best choice to prevent accidental shooting. Any llama used during hunting season should wear liberal amounts of florescent ribbon and cloth tied to halter, cinch, and tail, and even florescent pack saddles.

Toenails

Remember to check the llama's toenails before purchasing the animal. Although trimming toenails presents no great hardship, it does take time. For an idea of how often the llama's nails need trimming, ask to see the his health records. The rate of wear and the rate of growth of the toenail influence the frequency of trimming. If the llama often walks on abrasive surfaces, the toenail will wear down quickly. However, if the soil contains few rocks or is covered with snow much of the year, the nails will wear down slowly.

The rate of growth of the toenail is unique to each llama. Some llamas have faster growing toenails than others. Llama owners have no-ticed that light-colored toenails require more frequent trimming because they either grow faster or are harder and wear down more slowly than dark-colored toenails. Therefore, if you must choose between two otherwise equal males, select the one with dark toenails.

Pick up each of the llama's four feet and look at the toenails. Pay attention to how difficult or easy it is to pick up the foot. Most llamas do not want you to hold their feet, but will allow it with some resistance. Be sure to pick up all four feet; just because a llama allows you to pick up a front foot does not necessarily mean you can get anywhere near his rear legs.

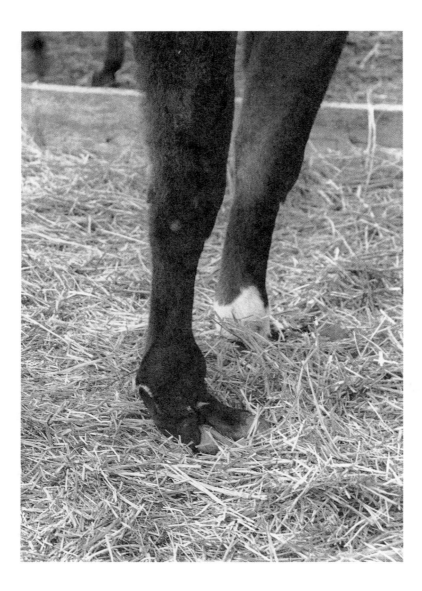

These overgrown toenails prevent the llama from standing properly and can permanently deform the llama's foot and leg.

Health and Conformation

Body build, personality, and degree of training mean nothing if a llama suffers from poor physical health or bad conformation. Health records and a careful visual inspection will reveal much about the general health of the llama.

Check the llama's health records for past serious illness, injuries, and occurrences of colic or bloat (uncommon in llamas). A llama with a history of injuries to the feet or legs should be eyed with great caution. When you visit the farm, watch the llama for signs of inactivity, limping, or heavy breathing (normal respiration rate is ten to thirty breaths per minute). Have the owner show you the bottom of the llama's feet—all four. Llamas with toenails overgrown to the point of curving back into the pad and excessively cracked pads should be avoided.

If the llama passes your initial check, ask your veterinarian to conduct a more detailed health examination before you purchase the

llama. This is important. Spend the $50 for a vet check even though the llama may look healthy.

We learned the hard way. We bought a seemingly healthy three-year-old gelded pack llama one fall with great expectations for the next summer pack season. By early spring we noticed Max breathing heavily while just standing around the barn and very reluctant to head out to pasture with the other llamas. In mid-April, our vet examined him and told us Max had severe heart disease and could die anytime. Max died the next day in the barn, and the autopsy confirmed congenital heart defects. A veterinarian could have detected this problem the previous fall if we had had Max checked before we purchased him.

We wrote earlier in this chapter on the preferred build for a pack llama. No matter what the build of a prospective llama—football player or basketball player—the parts need to be put together correctly. Think of the llama as a bridge and the llama's bones as the trusses that support

Pre-purchase vet inspection.

the bridge. If the trusses are incorrectly engineered, the bridge cannot support its load. Similarly, if a llama has a serious conformation fault, the pack llama will not be able to carry heavy loads over long distances.

The llama relies on its legs and feet for carrying heavy loads. Take care to purchase llamas with normal legs and feet, or only minor conformational faults.

In addition to specific conformation, the llama should appear balanced, and move easily. If the llama appears awkward, unbalanced, uncomfortable, or choppy in his movements, either eliminate the animal from consideration or review your observations with your vet. The more time you spend looking at llamas, the better you will become at judging an animal's conformation.

The Shopping Trip

Once you know what to look for in a pack llama, you can start shopping. Always keep a level head, noting what makes a good pack llama rather than falling in love with the first llama you see. Remember, the more llamas you see and the more llama owners you talk with, the better comparisons you can make and the more knowledgeable you will become.

There are three places to shop for llamas: at breeding farms or ranches, at farm liquidation sales, and at auctions. First-time llama buyers will find farm liquidation sales and auctions risky marketplaces because of the limited time one can spend with each llama, so we will focus first on the farm visit.

Visiting a farm or ranch gives you the time to get to know a llama and his owner and an opportunity to assess the llama's home environment. Visit at least three farms before choosing a llama—even if you eventually buy an animal from the first farm you visited. Three organizations can help you locate potential llama sellers (see Appendix). The International Llama Association (ILA), the Llama Association of North America (LANA), and the Canadian Llama Association (CLA) all publish membership directories listing the names, addresses, and phone numbers of members. A few phone calls to llama owners in your area will serve as your entree to the llama market.

When you first arrive at the farm, appraise the operation. Is the place neat and orderly, or is baling twine scattered among broken shovel handles and pop cans? A well-organized farm usually means organized husbandry and health practices. Don't jump to conclusions, but make a mental note of the appearance.

Explain to the owner that you are looking for a pack llama, or be prepared to see the entire herd. If you want to see the entire herd—males, females, and babies—that is fine. However, the more llamas you see, the more difficult it will be to remember the particular animal that interests you.

Before seeing the animals, collect as much information about the pack llamas for sale as you can. Minimal information should include age, gelding or stud, previous health record, and price. Do not pay too much attention to bloodlines unless you plan on breeding your llama. (Most of the famous studs are small woolly llamas who have never seen a pack.)

Keep in mind that llamas will continue to grow until around the age of three. Although a two-year-old llama can begin to pack, you must load him lightly for the first summer. A one-year-old llama can accompany the pack string as a training exercise, but should not be expected to carry weight. Just as young children with undeveloped muscles should not lift weights, so too should young llamas be allowed to develop before carrying a load.

When you finally get to the paddock containing the pack llama, observe the llama's activities. Try to get a feel for the personality of the llama. Ask the owner to halter and lead him out of the paddock. Watch carefully as the owner approaches the llama. Is the llama skittish about being approached? A skittish llama probably would be difficult to catch if loose in the woods. Is he head shy when the halter is put on? This is a difficult trait to correct, and a head-shy llama could hurt you if he throws his head. The perfect pack llama will offer little resistance to being cornered, and then will lay its ears back and fully submit to having its halter put on.

Ideally, you should take the llama on a short walk and, if you are seriously interested, plan a time to return to the farm for a more extensive outing with your future packing companion.

Shopping at an auction or farm liquidation sale usually does not give you time to carefully assess the llama. Most auctions have a show the day before the sale. The judge of the show,

however, is looking for specific breeding characteristics—qualities that may not make a good pack llama. Therefore, you will want to assess the llama yourself before the auction starts. Allow yourself as much time as possible, usually the day before the sale, to determine which, if any, of the llamas would make good pack stock and to decide on a maximum price. Do not let yourself get caught up in the excitement and hype of the auction—stick to that price and don't bid any higher!

One advantage of shopping at an auction or farm liquidation sale is the large selection of llamas in one central location, as auctions often represent twenty or more farms. Another advantage is that you can often buy pack llamas for a lower price at an auction. The trade-off is the risk associated with not knowing the llama or owner as well as if you had shopped at a farm. Your must choose whether the 10 to 20 percent savings at an auction is worth the risk. To the first-time buyer we suggest not risking it—stay clear of auctions.

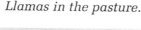

Llamas in the pasture.

After the Decision

Finding the perfect pack llama is challenging. Fortunately, most pack llamas prove adequate for most people. Once you have selected your llama, the hardest work is over, but a few chores remain before you bring your llama home.

If you have selected a llama from another state, province, or country, you will need to obtain the required health certificates for crossing borders before transporting him home. Before you bring your llama home, you should also pay a deposit, schedule a pre-purchase veterinary inspection, complete registration forms, and draft the bill of sale. Finally, you should agree upon and get in writing any guarantees the seller is offering regarding the animal's fitness for the purpose for which he is being sold. A pack llama should be fit to pack, and this can usually be determined prior to purchase through handling and an inspection by a qualified veterinarian. Most breeders will stand behind the stock they have raised, but be sure to get any guarantees in writing.

Health Inspections and Transportation

Certain health inspections, and even quarantine periods, are required when transporting livestock from one state, province, or country to another. Your local veterinarian can tell you which tests and certificates are needed. The seller may be willing to assume responsibility for providing the proper health certificates for traveling; however, the purchaser usually bears the costs for pre-purchase veterinary inspections and health certificates. These costs, often over $100, must be considered when shopping out-of-state or across the border.

If you have selected an animal from a distant ranch, transportation costs may also become significant. You and the seller must decide who

Finding the perfect pack llama is a challenge—remember personality is one of the most important characteristics of a good pack llama.

will deliver the llama to your place and whether the selling price includes transportation costs.

As we discussed earlier, it is wise to have a veterinarian examine your llama prior to purchase. Although people customarily have this done with more expensive breeding stock, it is also an excellent idea with a working animal that will be used for packing.

Insurance companies will provide insurance to protect against the risk of a motor vehicle accident and other named perils, or you can purchase more expensive full mortality insurance to protect against death due to accident or illness. The company will require a health certificate from a veterinarian before providing full mortality insurance. The Appendix lists insurance companies that provide this type of coverage.

Deposits

When you decide to purchase an animal, standard practice allows the seller to request a deposit. Even if the seller does not require one, it is generally a good idea to reserve the llama by placing a deposit. Your deposit demonstrates to the seller your serious intention to purchase that llama; in turn, your deposit obligates the seller to hold the animal until the agreed upon purchase date. A customary deposit covers about 10 percent of the purchase price.

Be sure to get a receipt for your deposit. The receipt should state that the seller reserves the llama for you to purchase by a certain date. It should also specify the terms of the sale, such as total purchase price, payment schedule, guarantees, and responsibility for transportation. The receipt can provide for contingencies as well, such as whether the deposit is refundable and under what conditions (for example, an unsatisfactory pre-purchase veterinary inspection or the llama's failure to pass the required health certification needed to cross a border). If none of the contingencies apply and you do not complete the purchase by the date specified in

the receipt, the seller is free to sell the animal to someone else, with no obligation to refund your deposit. If you are not able to bring the animal home within one or two months, you might explore the possibility of purchasing the llama and paying boarding fees to the seller until you are able to bring the animal home.

All parties involved should consider the deposit a preliminary step in the sale. The distinction between putting down a deposit and actually purchasing the llama is important. The seller owns the llama until you pay the balance of the purchase price and arrive to pick up the animal. Before this time, he or she assumes the risk of loss of the llama. If the llama becomes ill, is injured, or dies prior to your completing the purchase, your deposit should be refunded. The Appendix shows a sample purchase agreement including a deposit receipt.

Bill of Sale

When you pay the remainder of the purchase price and either pick up the animal or have it delivered, the seller should give you a bill of sale (see example in Appendix). The bill of sale acknowledges receipt of the purchase price, as well as giving the purchaser's name, seller's name, date of sale, and signature of seller. The bill of sale should also describe the llama, give its name, sex (male or gelded male), registration number (if registered), birthdate, and how it is being sold (as a pack animal, or "as is" without any warranty as to fitness for purpose). Some sellers include a warranty that, as the true owner, they have the authority to sell the llama. Some also include a copy of a photograph of the llama showing any distinctive markings.

Remember that many llama owners have no previous experience selling livestock and may not be familiar with these customary practices. Be sure to discuss the terms of the deposit and the terms of the bill of sale with the seller, and get it in writing before a problem arises.

Odds and Ends

Usually a llama is sold with a halter but not with a lead line. Double check this with the seller before you arrive without a halter to pick up the llama.

The seller should also provide complete health records for the llama, including dates of vaccinations, worming, toenail trimming, and any additional veterinary treatment such as castration and teeth trimming on mature animals. Without this information you will have to assume that none of it has been done and may unnecessarily duplicate medication.

If you are purchasing a registered llama, be sure to have the seller sign the proper place on the back of the registration certificate. The seller's signature allows the certificate to be transferred into your name. If the seller does not sign the certificate, you can submit a copy of the bill of sale to the International Lama Registry along with a request to transfer the certificate into your name. There is a nominal fee for the transfer of the certificate.

If you are purchasing an unregistered llama but may register him in the future, be sure to get information on the llama's genealogy. As of July 1992, the International Lama Registry registers only llamas whose parents are registered. Registering breeding stock is an important means of keeping track of genealogy. However, since most pack llamas are geldings, registering your llama may not concern you. The Appendix lists the address of the International Lama Registry.

Have the seller sign the registration form on the back.

– 5 –

TRAINING AND CONDITIONING

To be prepared for a full season of packing, your llama must know what you expect of him and be in shape to carry a pack. Training llamas to accept a pack and carry a load is easier than it might sound. They learn quickly and remember well. As long as you remain calm, patient, and consistent, most llamas will respond readily to training. Since there are probably as many theories of training as animals trained, we will outline techniques that have worked well for us. Most likely, you will adapt these techniques to your own situation.

Almost as important as the training is getting your llama in shape to do the work you expect of him. No matter how well trained your llama is, his heart, lungs, muscles, and feet need to be conditioned before you can have a successful pack trip.

Training

In training your llama, you are teaching him to trust you. Building trust begins as soon as you bring your llama home. Every time you calmly enter the barn to feed and do chores or sit quietly in the pasture, your llama grows more relaxed around you. Even after your llama is trained to lead, to load into a trailer, and to accept a pack, your relationship will continue to develop as you learn more about each other. Ultimately your pack llama will accompany you on many outings, and each outing will be an extension of the training process.

A llama packer must understand the great trust it takes for the llama to do a seemingly simple task. The llama already knows how to jump logs and walk through water. He knows how to enter a trailer and how to balance on three legs so you can examine his foot. The objective of training is to get the llama to do these things at your request. However, at first

Giving a llama a proper greeting will help build a trusting relationship. Place your hands behind your back, and gently lean towards the llama so he can smell you without feeling threatened.

your llama will not want to do these things, and for good reasons. As a cursorial animal, the llama's only real means of defense is running. When a llama allows someone to hold his foot or head (with a halter and lead line), he loses flight as a means of defense. It takes great courage and trust for a llama to allow you to do these things.

Eventually you must be able to lift your llama's foot to trim toenails and to check for cuts on the pad, but you should work up to this. First you need to build a trusting relationship with the llama.

First Steps

You can begin training your llama when he is only five or six months old. Llamas younger than six months have a short attention span,

making training difficult. Excessive handling of very young llamas can also foster the berserk male syndrome, a condition where a llama fails to distinguish the difference between himself and a person. As the llama grows older and begins to wrestle and stage mock fights with his peers, he will consider a person his peer and playmate. What is cute in a youngster is dangerous in a 200-pound yearling. Llamas suffering from the berserk male syndrome will jump on humans, knock them down, and attempt to wrestle for dominance. Gelding these llamas as weanlings sometimes decreases the rough play, but they still have no respect for humans and will be intractable, prone to spit, and difficult to pack. The best prevention is to handle young males minimally and to begin actual training sessions after your llama is five or six months old and weaned. By then he will know he is a llama.

Adult llamas generally learn faster, remember lessons better, and can tolerate longer training sessions than youngsters. If an adult male is calm and easy to halter, you should have no trouble taking him through the same training process as you would a young animal. However, because of his size, an adult llama may be difficult to halter and lead if he is scared. The older llama also may remember a traumatic experience with humans in the past, and it will take time and extra work to overcome that bad experience. If you are unable to halter your adult llama without risking injury to either you or the animal, seek professional assistance from an experienced llama trainer. Whatever you do, do not entrust your llama to the bronc buster down the road. Many horse-training techniques are simply not suited to llamas. Rough handling

At four months old, these young llamas have begun training with short desensitizing sessions. At six months old, they will receive a week of short daily lessons. When they are ready to wean from their mothers, they will have gone on walks alone and will follow willingly on the lead line.

of your llama will produce a deep-seated distrust of humans, causing more problems in the long run.

Regardless of your llama's age, keep your initial training sessions short; two short sessions are better than one long one. For the best results, set aside time during a particular week to repeat a ten- to fifteen-minute lesson once or twice each day. You will likely find that you need only two or three consecutive days to teach your llama to accept a halter and lead.

Try to make the training sessions positive experiences for both you and your llama. Remember, you are building trust so that when you ask your llama to cross a stream or jump a log on the trail, he will cooperate fully. By keeping stress at a minimum during training sessions, you avoid creating the sort of "bad experience" that hinders the learning process. If you feel that either your llama or you are headed toward a negative situation, stop the training session early. Although it is best to end the session on a good note, it is better to cut the session short than to let it become a negative experience.

Catching and Haltering

Begin your training with several lessons on catching. A small pen, stall, or barn works best for this lesson. Remove the other llamas from the pen so they don't distract the llama you are training. A ten-foot length of one-inch diameter, white plastic PVC pipe works well to push your llama into the work area. Walk slowly and deliberately toward your llama with your arms outstretched. He will likely walk into a corner. Observe your llama as he stands in the corner. What does his body language tell you? Is he poised for flight, or has he adopted a resigned stance with his ears slightly back? Once he has adopted this resigned stance, he has accepted the idea that you are going to approach him.

Approach slowly and calmly, talking quietly to him. Do not chase him around. Place an arm around his neck and stand close to him as you rub his neck and talk reassuringly. If he pulls away you can simply walk with him. When he stops resisting, release him and move away.

As an alternative to putting your arm around your llama's neck, you can catch your llama in a small pen using a light cotton lead line called a catch-rope. Lay one end of a light cotton lead line across the llama's withers. Then, holding the other end of the lead, cross in front of your llama so the lead loops around his neck. Pick up the loose end of the lead from your llama's back, and holding both ends of the lead, approach your llama and stroke his neck. After your llama accepts the presence of the rope, you can clip the lead line in a loop around his neck.

Both methods work well. The important things are to move with your llama when he walks, so you are not in a tug-of-war, and to accustom him to being touched on the neck and having you stand close to him. The advantage of the catch-rope is that it allows you to step toward him and stroke his neck, then step away without losing contact.

Repeat the catching and neck stroking several times in each lesson. Be sure to work from both sides. Repeat this lesson at least twice a day for several days until your llama appears calm and accepts your presence. Now you are ready to begin haltering.

Let your llama smell and see the halter before you use it in a lesson. Leave it in the hay trough or place it in a feed bucket with a little grain. It is a good idea to practice the haltering motions with your llama before you even have the halter in your hand. All your motions of putting on the halter should be slow and deliberate.

To begin haltering, catch your llama and rub his neck with the halter in your hand. Let him smell the halter. Stand alongside your llama, and with your arm around his neck, use both hands to grasp the cheek straps and hold the halter open in front him. Slowly raise the halter and slide it over your llama's nose. Continue to

Place your arm around the llama's neck and stand close against him. If he moves, simply walk with him, do not attempt to hold him in one place.

Hold the halter open, with your hands on the cheek straps.

Slowly move the halter onto your llama's nose. Note the placement of Amy's hands.

Continue to move slowly as you buckle the halter. Repeat the process in reverse, moving slowly, when you remove the halter.

move slowly as you slide the strap behind his ears and into the buckle or snap.

Llamas are sensitive about having anything on their faces, so you should give your llama a few minutes to get used to wearing the halter. Repeat your catching lessons several times, then remove the halter. To take the halter off, unbuckle it, but hold it together with your hand as if it were still buckled. Standing alongside the llama, slide your other arm around his neck. Place both hands back on the cheek straps on both sides of his face. Gently lift on both cheek straps so the noseband lifts up. Slowly slide the halter off your llama's face. Keep your arm around his neck until you are ready to release him. If your llama pulls away when you start to remove the halter, try using the catch-rope around his neck to hold him next to you.

If your llama has had a bad experience with a halter, you may need to spend more time on the haltering lessons. If he attempts to avoid the halter by raising his nose in the air or ducking away, you can counteract this by placing your arm higher around his neck and holding his neck snugly against your body in the crook of your arm. The catch-rope also can be placed high around his neck so that your llama cannot lift his head high in the air.

Be sure that the halter fits your llama and is neither too tight nor too loose. A loose halter will slide down onto the soft part of the nose and block the llama's breathing. If the halter needs adjustments, remove it, make the necessary changes, and start again. Halters usually come in different sizes: weanling (very small), small, medium, large, and extra large. A well-fitting halter for training will likely be too snug around the jaw to allow for normal cud chewing.

For safety and for your llama's comfort, always remove the halter before leaving your llama unattended. Your llama can get a foot caught in the halter or snag the halter in the fence. Do not leave a llama unattended if he is wearing a halter with a clip, rather than a buckle, as the clip can catch on a wire fence and cause your llama to panic.

Taking the Lead

Once your llama accepts the halter readily, you can begin leading him. There are many methods to teach a llama to lead. You could entice him to follow you almost anywhere with a can of grain, but what happens if you run out of grain in the backcountry? You could tie the lead to the bumper of a car and drag the llama into a walk. This method is even less practical, yet we've heard of someone trying this approach. We've also heard horror stories about people using electrical shocks and other pain-causing apparatuses to train animals. If you want to share your backcountry experiences with a companion, we suggest you build a bond with your llama based on trust—not on food, power, or pain.

Begin your leading lessons in an open area, as your llama may react at first with a few bucks and high-flying maneuvers when he realizes he has lost freedom of movement.

Although you will usually clip the lead line into the ring at the bottom of the noseband on the halter, in training simply place a cotton lead line around your llama's neck and clip it into itself. Make sure the rope is thick enough in relation to the clip that it will not tighten around the llama's neck. Some lead ropes have a metal ring to clip to, preventing the rope from tightening like a choker. You can easily make one of these yourself.

Your llama may act up after you clip the lead line around his neck. Move with him, letting him buck if he wants to. When he finishes bucking, move up the lead line, stroke his neck, and speak calmly to him. If you have been using the catch-rope technique, your llama will be fairly accustomed to having a rope around his neck while you handle him. We suggest using the lead around the neck for the first few leading lessons. We have found that the llama accepts

Proper handling of the lead line. Make a loop that will pull out of your hand in an emergency—never wrap the line around your hand.

the lead line around his neck more readily and gets less upset than when the lead is clipped into the halter.

For safety reasons, do not wrap the lead line around your hand. Instead, hold it folded back on itself. By following this rule you will avoid getting your hand caught in the rope should your llama decide to bolt. This rule applies whenever you are leading any llama, experienced or not, at home or on the trail.

The basic technique for teaching a llama to lead is called the pull-and-release method. If you are using a lead line clipped around his neck, place it fairly high, just behind the back of the halter, and make sure it will not tighten around his neck when you pull against it. Firmly pull the lead line toward you. When the

llama first feels you pulling he will resist. Hold the tension until the llama finally takes a step forward, then immediately release the tension. This pause between steps is important. The pause is a reward for stepping in the direction in which his head is pulled, and it increases your llama's trust. You will pull and release for each step. The first leading lesson should be short: across a paddock and back. In just a few lessons the llama will be following you around like a shadow. But remember, you did not teach the llama to walk. You taught him to trust you a bit—enough to follow you on the lead line.

As soon as your llama catches on to the idea of following you, you can venture out on a short journey or start taking short walks with someone else leading another llama. Keep these first walks short, perhaps just down the driveway. Your llama will be interested in his surroundings and will learn to follow you more readily. Watch what his behavior on these early outings: is he simply keeping up with his buddy, or is he really walking because you have trained him to follow? If you have questions, lead him in front of the other llama, or take him out alone. Make him stop, start, and even trot with you.

A properly trained pack llama should walk on a loose lead line, several feet behind the hiker. On a narrow trail, it would be dangerous for the llama to walk on the hiker's heels or constantly try to pass the hiker; and it would be irritating if the hiker must constantly pull the llama along. The llama should be able to adjust his speed to match the hiker's pace without pushing or lagging behind. Practice walking faster and slower with your llama. If your llama tries to pass you, swing the loose end of the lead line in a circle in front of you. This will usually discourage him from coming too close. You can also swing your free hand back and startle him by bumping him on his chest. If your llama is

setting a slow pace, swing your arm and hand holding the lead line in time to your walk. By swinging your arm as you walk, you are duplicating the pull-and-release method of training. If the llama keeps up, he is rewarded by not having a jerk on his head. If he slows down, the jerk encourages him to step out. A steady pulling does not accomplish nearly as much as the swinging arm.

We once worked with a young, energetic yearling male named Fitz Roy. On Fitz Roy's first hike, we had a friend lead him. We noticed that she kept him on a short lead, but Fitz Roy seemed well behaved and walked alongside her on the way out. However, when we turned around to head home, there was absolutely no keeping him back. The harder she pulled back, the more anxious he was to pass her. After he jumped up on his hind legs in his anxiety to pass her, Amy decided to take over. First, Amy tried swinging the lead line in a circle in front of her, but Fitz Roy just walked through it. Every time he passed her, she made him walk in a small circle so he was back behind her. In the

A well-trained llama should follow easily on a loose lead.

process, Amy and Fitz Roy passed several llamas until they were first in line.

By this time, we had descended the steepest part of the slope, so Amy tried relaxing and giving Fitz Roy a longer lead line. Presto! He responded by relaxing, dropping back, and walking behind as a well-behaved llama should. After a few minutes of calm walking, we made the mistake of turning the lead line back to the first leader. Used to working with horses, she shortened up on his lead line again, leaving only about two feet between his head and her hand. Within moments Fitz Roy was again trying to dart ahead, getting increasingly agitated with each attempt. Amy took over again, and immediately gave him the full six feet of lead. Fitz Roy (now called Schiz Roy for his quick personality changes) calmly walked the rest of the way home. It was interesting that the harder we tried to control him on a short lead, the more wound up he became. Loosening the lead worked wonders in relaxing him and easing our return to the barn.

Building Trust: Obstacle Training

Although some repetition enhances training, beware of boring your llama to the point that he does not want to be led. Keep your llama's interest by taking him to different places. The trick here is to find an obstacle challenging enough to test the llama, but not too difficult for him to overcome. Each new experience will build your llama's trust in you.

Start by walking your llama on a different surface, such as pavement or cement. As you approach the obstacle, give him a few seconds to smell and observe the pavement. Pull, and when he puts his first foot on the pavement, release. Use this same technique to get the llama over other obstacles, such as low logs, bridges, and small creeks.

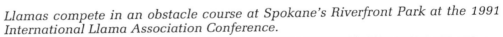

Llamas compete in an obstacle course at Spokane's Riverfront Park at the 1991 International Llama Association Conference.

Next you might try leading your llama into a confined area, such as a garage or your house. By taking him into a tight space, you are eliminating possible escape routes, so the llama will be reluctant to enter. Repeat this exercise several times until he does not hesitate at the entry way.

The greater variety of situations your llama experiences without trauma, the more trust he will have in you. Although it is preferable to surmount each obstacle you ask your llama to face, that is not always possible. If you misjudge and approach an obstacle that he is not ready for, accept that and go back to something you know he is comfortable doing.

After four or five successful encounters, your llama should have mastered an obstacle and you can move on. Moving away from familiar surroundings is the best way to maintain his interest level. Your llama will enjoy getting out into the woods, or even walking around the neighborhood, and he will learn more there than you can possibly teach him at home.

Desensitizing and Grooming

The traditional idea of grooming, as it relates to horses or dogs, does not apply to pack llamas. Llamas generally avoid excessive physical contact with each other in the pasture and naturally do not appreciate having humans touch them. When humans approach them with a wire brush in hand and proceed to rip their wool out by the roots, it is no wonder they react strongly, kicking or spitting. You will therefore want to desensitize your llama before you attempt to brush or clean him.

You can peel loose wool off a molting llama using a round pet rake (a dog grooming tool).

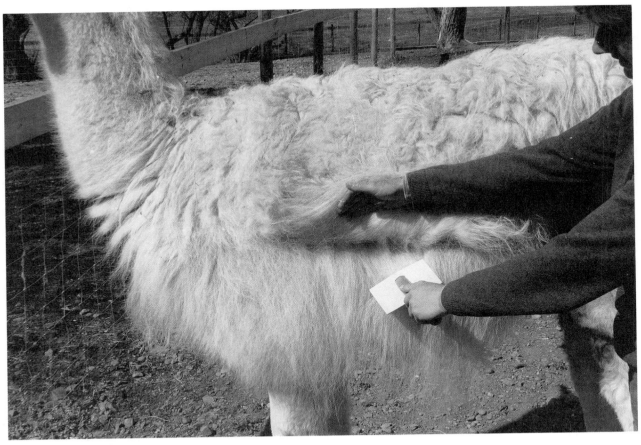

A slicker brush, normally used on dogs, works well to remove debris and loose wool. However, excessive use of a slicker brush can break fibers and damage the llama's wool.

The TTEAM (Tellington-Jones Equine Awareness Method) training method, originally developed for horses, strives to create a non-stressful training environment for you and your llama. We highly recommend attending a clinic and incorporating the TTEAM philosophy into your training and handling of llamas. TTEAM advocates letting your llama loose in a small pen or box stall and using two dressage whips as wands to desensitize him, rather than touching him directly with your hands. (See the Appendix for references and addresses for more information on TTEAM training clinics.) You may want to put down fresh hay or grain to relax him between exercises. Work the two wands in unison to stroke the llama's neck (front and back simultaneously), then back and belly, and finally the front of the front legs at the same time as the back of the back legs. Consistent use of these wands in short, ten-minute sessions begins the desensitization process. The llama will more readily allow you to touch him with your hands after he has accepted the wands. With your llama loose in the small pen, proceed to touch him by hand and then to brush him. If he is jumpy, and nervous about your touching him, go back to using the wands for several more sessions. Pay special attention to desensitizing the areas where the pack saddle and cinch will lie. Each time you prepare to put the pack on, you will want to touch your llama to check the saddle area for large thistles, burrs, sticks, or other possible irritants. You will also want to be able to touch the front and rear armpits and to run your hand down the belly without alarming your llama.

The first step in grooming is to use an electric leafblower to remove dirt and loose debris. Stand six or seven feet from your llama and direct the air away from his head so that dust will not blow into his eyes. Your llama will quickly grow accustomed to the sound and feel of the blower. Blow the llama's wool for ten to fifteen minutes, then either brush or shear his wool. You can buy a leafblower for several hundred dollars through llama equipment catalogs, or you can go down to Sears and get the same thing at a fraction of the cost.

After blowing away the debris, tie your llama on a very short lead to a secure fence using a quick-release knot, or turn him loose in a 10 x 10 stall. (See Appendix for directions on tying a quick-release knot.) Make sure the llama cannot injure himself on the fence and that other llamas cannot disturb him. Using a short slicker brush or bristle brush, begin brushing the areas that are most acceptable to the llama, such as the neck and shoulders, and then move on to areas that are less acceptable.

Use firm brush strokes, but do not yank on the wool. Part the wool and brush down, away from the part, working on small sections at a time. Don't worry about getting every bit of debris out, just remove burrs and twigs that could cause pain under the cinch or pack saddle.

For llamas with thick, matted, or especially long wool that collects debris, we suggest either shearing the wool to two to four inches or waiting to see if your llama will molt. Llamas molt every two to three years, and the undercoat can then be removed without pulling. If there is considerable debris where the pack saddle lies, you may be forced to shear.

Some llamas are more sensitive than others to having their wool pulled. If your animal gets very upset by the brushing, you are probably

Pewter looks rather svelte after receiving his spring body clip in preparation for the packing season.

ripping out his wool by the roots, causing him considerable pain. If your llama acts as if he is in pain, do not continue.

Many llamas will groom themselves by rubbing against trees and brush in their pastures. These animals may only need a quick check for debris in their saddle and cinch areas prior to packing. We have often wondered if llamas would use a grooming post in the pasture. We plan to experiment by mounting stiff brushes at shoulder height in the barn.

One summer we spent several hours readying our large stud, McGruder, for the fair. His pasture contained some bushes, so he tended to keep himself groomed by passing through the brush. Although we did not bathe him, we did use the blower, brushed him thoroughly, sprayed him with a coat conditioner (for horses), and brushed him again. When we thought we were finished, Amy patted him on his back. Surprise! She felt a hard object and pulled a two-foot stick from under his wool.

Discipline: Achieving a Balance

Verbal praise offered in a soothing voice, release on a tight lead when the llama follows your command, and a small amount of grain or being turned out to pasture after a good training session all provide excellent positive reinforcements that will virtually eliminate the need for discipline. However, when a situation calling for discipline does arise, you should look first at the cause of the behavior.

Before you jump to discipline your llama for misbehaving, you should examine whether the llama is reacting from fear. If so, forceful discipline will only exacerbate the problem. Try instead to anticipate the point where your llama becomes scared and stop short of forcing him into this behavior. For example, if your llama kicks when you run your hand past a certain point on his hindquarters, repeatedly run your hand down his back, stopping just short of the point where he reacts. Repeat this for one or two minutes, each time extending the distance. Gradually he will permit you to touch more and more of his hindquarters as he gets accustomed to the feel of your touch. If he does kick, it is usually best to ignore it and continue. Your llama is hoping that his kicking will make you stop touching him. Ignoring his kicking teaches them that it does not make you stop what you are doing. Spitting can also indicate fear and loss of control due to that fear. Again it would be best to stop short of pushing the llama to the point of spitting, and if he does spit, ignore it so that the llama does not learn that spitting works.

If the llama is genuinely misbehaving, an immediate strong verbal reprimand, such as "NO!," is usually appropriate. You may also give a quick, sharp downward jerk on the halter as you say "NO!" Llamas are generally impervious to a slap on the side, and you should never strike a llama around the head as it will cause him to become head-shy.

Several books (see Appendix) provide written instruction on llama training. If you are having problems controlling your llama, these additional sources will help you solve them.

Introducing the Pack

At this point you should feel that your llama trusts you. He follows you willingly through all the obstacles, walks along on short hikes, and allows you to touch him on his neck, back, and belly. The next step is to introduce the pack.

While you were building the llama's trust, you also were getting him accustomed to your touch. Stroking and patting the llama around the less-sensitive nape of the neck and mid-back reinforces the idea that being touched is not a prelude to death. While on a leading exercise, tie a coat or sweat-shirt around the llama's neck and continue walking. Tie the clothing so it will not slip and touch the llama's sensitive front legs. Once the llama ignores the clothing, he is ready to start sacking out.

Sacking out is simply a more advanced form of the tied-on clothing. The trainer introduces pack-like material, nylon or canvas, and places it in the normal pack position on the llama's back. The introduction of the material is very important. Before throwing anything on the llama's back, allow him to see, hear, and smell the object. Slowly walk up to the llama's face with the material and allow the llama to inspect it. Nylon and other synthetic materials can make a lot of noise; rub the material together so the llama can see the source of that strange noise. Once he has satisfactorily inspected the material, rub it on his neck and gradually work it to the middle of his back.

Fold the sacking-out material so that it will not touch the llama's legs when he walks. The material should be heavy enough that a few quick side-steps will not send it flying. Slide the material on and off several times, and even allow the material to slip to the ground. Take your llama for a short walk so that he gets used to moving with material on his back.

Many llamas need to sack out only once, before you can move on. Others may need several sessions before they get used to the feel of the fabric. Don't rush this stage, the llama needs time to get used to the sound of fabric rustling on his back.

Once the llama is indifferent to the sack, standing or walking, you can introduce him to the pack. Follow the same procedure for putting on the pack as you did for sacking out. First detach all rigging that might dangle against the llama's sensitive legs. If your pack has both a front and rear cinch, remove the rear cinch for now. Until the llama becomes desensitized around the stomach, he probably will not like having the rear cinch placed under his belly. Allow your llama to see, hear, and smell the pack. Rub it against his neck and slowly slide the pack into position on his back. The first time you put on the pack, have a friend stand on the other side of the llama to pass the cinch under the belly to you. Position the front cinch just behind the front armpits of the llama. It should not interfere with the back-and-forth movement of the front legs. If the pack is designed properly, its center will ride just in front of the middle of the llama's back, with the cinch just behind the front armpits. This distributes most of the weight to the front legs where it should be.

Once you have a trusting relationship with your llama, and he readily accepts the pack, you can train him to allow children to ride on his back.

Tighten the cinch just enough to ensure that the pack will not slide or rotate if the llama should go into a jumping frenzy. As you fasten the cinch, place your hand under the cinch against the llama's belly to be sure no wool gets caught up in the rigging or buckle. Llamas do not like to have their wool pulled, and you do not want your llama to associate wearing a pack with the pain of having wool pulled.

With the pack in place, walk your llama to get him accustomed to moving with it. The pack will bounce, make noise, and feel strange to the llama. More than likely, his reaction will be slight. A more skittish llama, however, may throw a small fit. To prepare yourself for action, have the llama in an open area free of objects for

him to get hurt on, and use a cotton lead to reduce rope burn for you and the llama. If the llama should act up, simply hang on until he is through jumping. Once he gets back to his senses, start walking again.

Usually after a few short walks with the saddle on, you can attach the panniers. Give your llama a chance to get used to each new step in the process: first the front cinch, then both front and rear, then panniers, then loaded panniers, and finally, as a more advanced move, tying your llamas together to form a string.

We recently received a phone call from a fellow who was convinced that his llama would never become a pack llama. He had put a pack saddle on his llama for the first time that day.

Stringing along. Once your llamas become accustomed to walking in a string, they will prefer it and make better time on the trail.

The llama stood so well that he figured, "What the heck?" and attached the panniers. Everything had progressed so smoothly that he thought he could take his other llama along for a walk at the same time, so he tied the second llama onto the back of the pack. Then he untied the first llama and led him through the gate.

Predictably, when the fabric of the pack rubbed against the gate, the llama went temporarily insane, smacking his head against the fence post, and bucking into the middle of the yard. The owner was forced to let go, and the poor llama tied behind had no choice but to follow as best he could. The llama quickly wore himself out, allowing his owner to catch him. Luckily for everyone, this unfortunate experience resulted in nothing more serious than a rope burn for the owner and a split lip for the llama.

We reassured the owner that his llama was reacting in a perfectly normal way under the circumstances, and we suggested he back up to the sacking out phase and wait a while before tying llamas together. He looked at us in disbelief when we told him that, after about five minutes on a trail, his llama will likely forget he is wearing a pack. We have recently heard that, although they have not yet ventured out onto the trail, the two llamas regularly tour the neighborhood, tied together and wearing packs.

Lifting the Foot: The Ultimate Trust

Now that your llama accepts a halter, follows you on a lead line, and wears a pack, you are almost ready to hit the trail. Your llama trusts you enough to allow you to touch him on his neck and back and belly; you are ready to attempt to lift his foot. Being able to lift your llama's foot allows you to check or trim his toenails, and in the event of injury, treat his foot pad.

Tie your llama securely to a fence with a quick-release knot on a very short lead. Start by desensitizing the area where the front leg at-taches to the body. Standing alongside your llama and facing the tail, gradually work your hand down the front leg. Should your llama start to dance, simply keep your hand firmly against his body and speak calmly to him. When he stops dancing, proceed. If you have done preliminary work with the TTEAM wands, your llama will be desensitized already. Once he accepts your touch below the knee joint, lean against his shoulder to shift his weight off the foot, then lift. Hold his foot at the ankle joint. The first few times you lift his foot, simply touch the toes and pads, then gently place the foot back on the ground. It is rude and inconsiderate, as well as bad training, to drop the foot suddenly.

Do not allow your llama to lean half his weight on you as a condition of letting you hold his foot. If he starts to sag against you, move so that you are not supporting any weight, only holding onto his foot. He will then need to shift his weight to the other three legs while you work on the one foot.

Move to the back legs and repeat the desensitizing process. Again, face the back of your llama as you run your hand down his leg. Stand as close as possible, actually touching your llama to lessen the threat of a kick. If you stand right against your llama, it is much harder for him to kick with any force. If your llama particularly dislikes having his back legs touched, begin with desensitizing a hind leg, then move on to the other front leg. It may take several days of handling before he is comfortable giving you all four legs. Once he is comfortable with you handling his feet, you can trim his toenails and examine the tough leathery pads so that you will notice any changes. You now have a trained pack llama.

Work with your llama in several short ten minute sessions. Whenever you sense you or your llama getting worked up, it is time to quit. As he becomes more accustomed to you handling him, you can work in longer sessions.

Dave leans against Kachina's shoulder to shift her weight off her front foot as he slides his hand down her leg.

Dave gently, but firmly, grasps the fetlock and lifts Kachina's leg.

Dave repeats the process on the back leg: leaning against Kachina to shift her weight, and sliding his hand down her leg. He stands close to her to prevent kicking.

Dave lifts the back leg and holds it out, ready for trimming. Although he allows the llama to balance against him, he expects her to support her own weight.

Getting In Shape

One of the most important aspects of successful llama packing is adequate conditioning—getting in decent physical shape before heading for the hills. What good is a llama that can jump logs and cross creeks if he is too out of shape to make it up the first hill? Good conditioning enables you to reach a reasonable destination on time without undue stress or injury to you or your llama.

A few years ago we did a four-day trek with some friends who also own llamas. The first day was a disaster. After hiking only three miles, our friend's llama lay down on a steep section of trail and refused to get up. We got him up for a few seconds and could tell from his shaky legs and general appearance that he was exhausted—and after only three miles!

The llama needed at least a few hours rest and we still had hours of hiking ahead to reach camp before nightfall. We decided if we could urge the llama down to the base of the hill some members of our group would make camp there and the rest of us would continue on.

Two days later we returned to our friends at the base of the hill, and the llama was doing fine. We all had to pitch in to pack out supplies that the out-of-shape llama would have carried, but we exited with all the gear and llamas we entered with. Needless to say our friends had a less than successful trip because they hadn't conditioned their llama before hitting the trail.

If your llama packs year-round or gets daily exercise (for instance, a gelding in a pen with an aggressive stud), the need for conditioning is minimal. Where the climate or other factors limit the pack season or the level of activity, the llama will need reconditioning after each period of inactivity. Llamas are very much like humans in this respect. Most of us wouldn't think of running a marathon or climbing a peak without an extensive training period beforehand. How can we expect more of our llamas?

Pre-season conditioning is a lot easier with the help of a neighbor's horse.

73

A Three-part Program

Llama conditioning falls into three categories: the feet, the muscles, and the respiratory system. Before going on any backcountry excursion ask yourself if your llamas have all three parts conditioned. If your llama has been sitting around the barn all winter, he will need complete conditioning. If your llama has a hilly pasture and gets plenty of exercise, he may be in shape already. If the answer is no, do yourself and your llama a favor and delay the trip until the llama is ready.

For all the advantages of the llama's foot, there is one drawback. The round leather pad on the bottom of the foot must be toughened before it can withstand heavy use. Sharp rocks and gravel common on most trails can cut unconditioned feet. In arid climates the pads face extremely high surface temperatures and the poking of cactus thorns.

The principle behind conditioning the foot is the same for humans and llamas. As kids our first barefoot excursions in the spring usually left us hobbling over the smallest of pebbles. This tenderness resulted from many months of our pale-white feet contacting only the soft lining of boots and shoes. After a month of running around barefoot our tanned, callused feet carried us painlessly over hot pavement and around the bases at the local ball park. Similarly an inactive llama spends a lot of time standing on the soft earth or with his feet tucked under his belly while sitting. To toughen his feet for packing, introduce him gradually to rougher walking surfaces.

A llama's muscles require preparation for packing a heavy load into the backcountry. When conditioning the muscles remember you need to exercise the exact muscles that will be used later. A person can run ten miles a day and think he's in great shape until he tries to row a boat or go skiing. If you want to be in shape for rowing a boat—row a boat. If you want your llama to be in shape to pack—pack a load on him and go for a hike.

It's easy to overlook the third aspect of conditioning—the respiratory system. You might think you're ready to hit the trail after watching your llama walk five miles around the house. But what's going to happen on the first hill where he really needs to work? A llama can have excellent muscle and foot tone, but he

Willing friends volunteer for early spring conditioning hikes. Start without packs and work up to heavier loads.

won't be worth a small woolly alpaca under a saddle if you haven't conditioned him aerobically. The normal llama respiratory rate is 10-30 breaths per minute. You need to get his respiratory rate up (get him breathing hard) and get him used to working with an elevated breathing rate. Your llama should be able to function for 10 minutes at a time at 50 breaths per minute.

Start Early and Start Slowly

The keys to a good conditioning program are to start early and to start slowly. Your llama's initial fitness and your fitness goals for him determine how much conditioning he needs. Some llamas take less time to get in shape than others. Adjust your schedule to your llama's needs, but don't make the mistake of starting fitness training just a week before your first outing. It's not enough time.

A trick for getting yourself in shape and to keep you from overworking your llama is for you to carry a backpack on the conditioning walks. Put the same percentage of your body weight in your backpack as you are putting in the llama's panniers. If the llama is carrying 10 percent of his body weight, you carry 10 percent of yours. If you find yourself gasping for air midway up a hill, look over your shoulder and check the llama. He may also need a short break.

Our pack string does nothing from mid-November to late spring. We monitor their body weights monthly and expect their weight to increase by about 15 percent over the winter. We start our pre-season conditioning about a month before our first trip. The following is a rough outline of our four-week pre-season conditioning schedule. Use it as a guide, realizing that your needs and the needs of your llama may differ from ours.

WEEK ONE: We spend the first week walking our llamas daily with a saddle attached but no weight in the panniers. Each day the walk becomes longer and more arduous. We start at

Carrying a pack on your own back as you condition your llama will help both of you get in shape.

a mile or two and work up to five miles, making an effort to condition foot pads by walking on abrasive surfaces such as gravel or pavement. You can assess your llama's body condition by monitoring his breathing. Watch his nostrils. They will flare and contract when he becomes fatigued. If you are not getting the nostrils to flare (not increasing his respiratory rate), you are not giving him a good aerobic workout. If he needs to hold his mouth open to breathe (assuming he hasn't just been in a spitting match), he's working too hard—stop and let his breathing return to normal. Try to keep the same pace all week even though the distances are getting longer; otherwise you'll find a slug, not a llama, in the halter. If you have more than one llama to condition, string them together to save you time.

Creating a String

When several llamas are tied together, one behind the other, you have what is called a pack string. Start with a llama who is a good leader. You lead the first llama after using a quick-release knot to tie the second llama's lead line to the pack saddle of the first llama. There is usually a loop in the center back of the pack saddle for this purpose. For fast release, you can put a metal carabineer through the loop and tie the lead line around the metal. Once the two llamas are used to being tied together, practice leading the second llama and tying a third llama to that one. Soon you will be able to string several llamas together and condition them all at once as you gradually increase the weight they are carrying.

When stringing llamas together, be sure you can always untie the llamas quickly with a quick-release knot in case they panic or get tangled. For additional safety tie a thong of leather or other breakable material, which you know will break under extreme pressure, between the saddle and the carabineer. (See photo page 112.)

Although you can pack with llamas as young as 18 months, you should load them lightly. Gallatin is carrying only sleeping bags and pads on his first trip out.

WEEK TWO: Assuming satisfactory progress in week one, we begin placing weight in the panniers in the second week. The most we pack on our llamas is 25 percent of their in-condition body weight. Our goal for this and the next two weeks is to work up to that weight. Start with 10 percent of your llama's body weight in the panniers. Because the weight puts more stress on their muscles, we only work them every other day. This gives them a day to rest and recuperate before the next workout. Again we start out at two miles and work up to five miles. Half-way through the week, after two or three workouts, increase the load to 15 percent of their body weight and continue.

For very short distances, the mature llama can carry up to 35 percent of his body weight. Over long distances or long durations, however, 25 percent of his body weight is maximum. Immature, one- and two-year-olds should never carry more than 20 percent of their body weight. A safe weight to start with is 10 percent of their body weight. Once the llama has adjusted to this weight, increase it in 5 percent increments until you reach the maximum weight for that llama.

The table below gives you a general idea of a llama's maximum pack weight based on his age and in-condition body weight.

This chart assumes a llama in prime condition and that you know his optimal body weight.

Using the 25 percent figure, you would assume that your 400-pound llama could carry 100 pounds. If your llama is 50 pounds overweight, his true body weight is 350 pounds, and he is already carrying 50 pounds of fat. Your llama could actually carry 25 percent of 350 pounds, which is only 87 pounds. Since he is already carrying the extra 50 pounds of fat, he would be fully loaded with only 37 pounds of gear. Furthermore, if a llama is 50 pounds overweight, he is not in condition. You cannot expect him to carry a full load of 87 pounds until he is in better shape. In this case, your llama might be working very hard to carry just 25 pounds of gear.

Remember, the load your llama will carry for you depends on a number of factors—body weight being only one. External conditions such as temperature, terrain, and amount of wool are fairly easy to judge. Personality, body type, conditioning, and willingness to work are also major factors which are harder to assess. Experience with your animals, combined with a good livestock scale for monthly records of weight gain or loss, will help you determine the appropriate load for each of your llamas.

WEEK THREE: Your llama should be getting in the groove by now. Increase the load to 20 percent of his body weight and walk him from two up to five miles. Boredom may set in if you go over the same trail every session. Vary the

AGE	WEIGHT	MAXIMUM PACK WEIGHT
1 year	180 to 240 pounds	18 to 24 pounds
2 years	240 to 340 pounds	24 to 34 pounds
3 years	280 to 390 pounds	40 to 80 pounds
4 years	280 to 440 pounds	56 to 110 pounds
over 4	280 to 440 pounds	70 to 110 pounds

scenery and try to make the workouts fun. Fun for a llama is food, so stop in lush areas and let him graze for a bit. Make sure you are the one who initiates the stop. When you get back to the barn reward your llama with a handful of grain for his efforts.

WEEK FOUR: This week's workouts separate the *crias* from the *padres*. Increase the load to 25 percent of your llama's body weight and continue to work him every other day. If he didn't handle last week's load well, do not increase it this week. Some of my llamas are not ready for the 25 percent load until mid-summer, and some never carry that much weight comfortably. Many factors go into determining what a llama will carry for you. Although his physical condition is important so is his personality, age, weight, and body build. With experience you will learn what each of your llamas can carry comfortably.

Adequate and thorough llama conditioning is vital to successful llama packing. If you've done the work before the trip, you'll enter the backcountry with confidence. You'll see more and enjoy more of the beauty in the backcountry if you are not worrying about whether your llama will even make it to camp.

Llamas, such as these in Peru, subsist on a very low protein diet. North American llamas may become overweight grazing on lush pastures.

– 6 –

PACKING EQUIPMENT

Eight years ago, if you had asked a tack shop employee where you could buy a llama pack or halter, he or she would have laughed at you. The only packs available were homemade. The early, homemade equipment became the prototypes for what today is a growing market. The Appendix lists several reputable llama equipment dealers.

Before getting into the nuts and bolts of llama packing equipment, we issue a warning about the quantity and sophistication of equipment. With the llamas carrying the load, you can pack more gear and supplies into the backcountry. But before you start shoving all those neat gadgets into your pack, stop and think about why you go camping in the backcountry. One reason is probably that camping allows you to live closer to nature. You leave behind much of the technological dazzle that usually clogs the senses back home. The sun replaces fluorescent lights; the buzz of a bee replaces the hum of electric motors. Remember this as you choose your equipment. Making do with a minimum of creature comforts will provide the most rewarding wilderness experience.

Halters and Leads

The first piece of equipment you'll purchase is a good halter. Although many llama halters are available, a good packing halter is made of nylon and is a fixed size (not adjustable). Nylon lasts longer than leather and can be thrown in the washer if necessary. Fancy, adjustable halters have too many moving parts, which can chafe the llama's face, and easily come out of adjustment. Buy a halter that fits your llama and mark it for that llama only. The only adjustable hardware on the halter should be one heavy-duty, double-bar buckle attaching the ends of the halter that run behind the ears. Halters with a spring-snap or crown buckle should not be used—they break easily. For that matter, any halter can break, so always take along one spare halter on the trail.

A snug-fitting halter works best while training a llama. Place the noseband high on the nose, just below the eyes, and make sure the halter is tight enough that it will not ride down on the soft part of the llama's nose, impairing

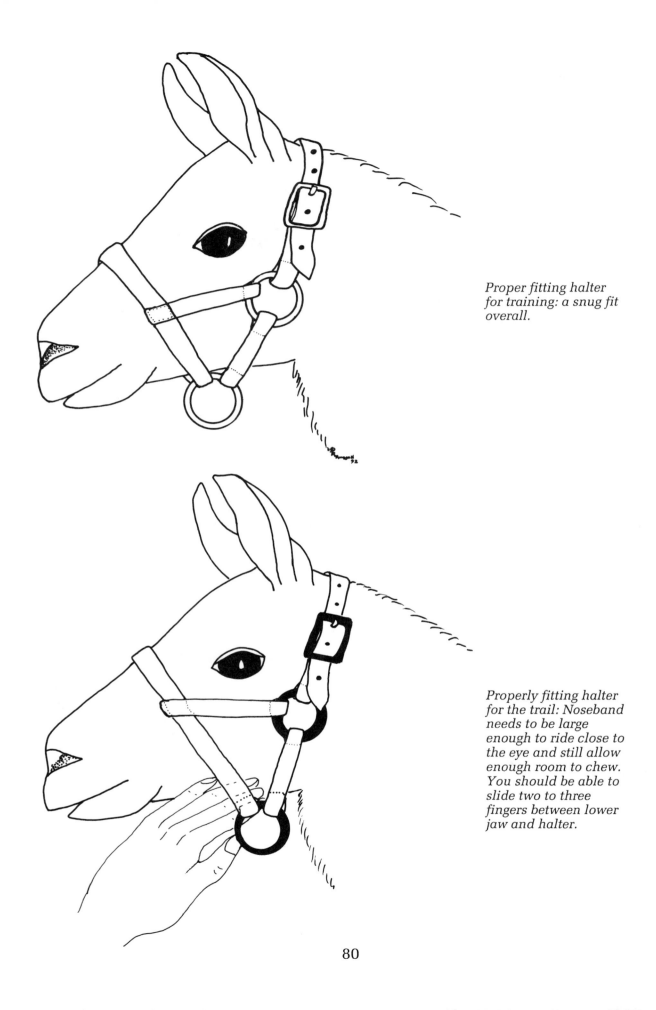

Proper fitting halter for training: a snug fit overall.

Properly fitting halter for the trail: Noseband needs to be large enough to ride close to the eye and still allow enough room to chew. You should be able to slide two to three fingers between lower jaw and halter.

his breathing. On the trail you want a looser fitting halter. Your llama will be wearing it for a number of days, so the halter must allow him room to chew his cud. We like to have an inch of sag in the noseband strap below the llama's lower jaw. With the noseband placed high on the llama's nose, just below his eyes, you should be able to insert two fingers under the noseband on a well-fitting halter for the trail. Our llamas wear halters one size larger on the trail than they wear in training at home.

The lead line that attaches to the halter should be durable. For training, a cotton lead works best because it is less apt to inflict rope burns. The durability of nylon, however, makes it a better choice for the trail. Also, tight knots are easier to tie and untie in the nylon lead. An eight- to ten-foot lead allows plenty of room between you and the llama without being long enough to trip over. Diameters of three-eighths to three-quarters of an inch fit the hand well and provide plenty of strength.

Cotton lead lines work best for training. Nylon leads will give you a rope burn if the llama pulls away from you.

Packs

To go llama packing you will need a llama pack. That point may appear obvious, but we know some folks who have tried to retrofit horse and mule packs to llamas, and it just does not work. Why should it? The llama's back is a different size and shape than that of a horse or mule. Many good llama packsaddles are available on the market today; the one for you will depend on your specific needs.

Llama packs come in two styles: the soft-saddle pack system and the hard-saddle pack system. Both systems consist of a saddle that attaches to the llama and two pack bags, or panniers, that attach, one on each side, to the saddle. The saddle secures to the llama with front rear cinches, both of which run under the llama's abdomen. For mountainous terrain, the saddle may have an optional breast strap and some form of rear strap to keep the saddle from slipping forward or backward. If the rear strap rides under the tail it is called a crupper; if it rides on the rump it is called a breeching.

The idea for hard-saddle pack system undoubtedly originated with the sawbuck, the original horse and mule packsaddle. Many llama owners use a sawbuck, or a variation, on their llamas. The biggest advantage of a sawbuck is that just about anything can be attached to the easily accessible cross-arms. The panniers range from wooden boxes to Coleman coolers. The only requirement is that each pannier needs two straps to loop over the cross-arms.

The llama in front is wearing the soft-saddle system, which is excellent for carrying clothing, food buckets, and sleeping bags. The llama behind is wearing a rigid sawbuck saddle, which works well for bulky loads such as these kitchen boxes.

Sawbuck saddles require special rigging to hold them in place: two cinches, breast strap, and breeching strap or crupper.

When hiking in rugged terrain, a breeching strap helps hold bulky kitchen loads in place.

David Harmon poses as a llama for a demonstration by Peruvian llama packers. The costal *(burlap sack) is filled, sewn shut, and then secured to the back of the llama with the* soga, *a braided rope made of llama wool. The* soga *wraps around the belly and over the llama's back.*

The standard wooden sawbuck has its problems, however. It is heavy, and the smooth curved bars that contact the llama do not conform well to the llama's back. You can shape the bars for a better fit, but with so much wool in the way it is hard to assess a good fit. Also, once shaped to a particular llama, it only fits that one llama. Variations on the sawbuck are much improved. Combinations of wood and light-weight metal allow for numerous adjustments and a better fit that can be readjusted easily for any llama.

The soft saddle traces its roots to the llama's homeland. For thousands of years, the llama herders of Peru and Bolivia have used a frameless pack bag called a *costal* that they secured to the llama with a long wool rope, or *soga*. The

costales that we saw on our 1991 trip to Peru were small burlap sacks. The sack was filled with potatoes or other goods, sewn shut, and then tied onto the llama's back by wrapping a rope around the body of the llama several times. In *costales*, llamas carried loads significantly lighter than those you might put on your llama, somewhere around 20 to 40 pounds.

The traditional *costal* places weight directly on the spine of the llama. Modern packers developed a soft frame that keeps the weight off the llama's spine, allowing him to carry heavier loads. When you go out and spend a small fortune for any of the "ultimate" llama pack-saddles on the market, think back to the simple burlap sack that has worked for thousands of years.

This soft packsaddle has padding to protect the llama's spine. Belly cinches fasten with Velcro and are easily adjustable. Panniers hold two square food buckets and hook easily to brackets on the saddle.

The soft saddles on the market today distribute the weight equally along the loins of the llama. The substitution of dense padded foam for the wooden bars of the sawbuck eliminates the problem of crossbars not conforming to the llama's shape. As you might guess, the soft-saddle system is lighter than most hard-saddle systems. A soft-saddle system works well for carrying clothing, sleeping bags, tents, and food buckets inside the panniers.

There are problems, however, with the soft-saddle system. Without the cross-arms to attach to, the panniers need to buckle, clip, or hang on the saddle. It is difficult to hold a loaded pannier and connect the four or more buckles or clips that attach it to the saddle. We much prefer panniers that can easily be hung on brackets.

One final consideration about panniers and packs is color. More people use the backcountry each year, underscoring the importance of blending with the surroundings. There is nothing worse than waking up in what you thought was a secluded area and seeing a bright orange tent across the meadow. Brightly colored llama panniers can cause the same disturbance. When you have a choice, buy earth-tones.

So which pack is for you? Fortunately most of the packs on the market will work in most conditions, and their construction protects the llama's backbone and spine. If you are not sure what loads you will be carrying and will buy only one pack, buy a hard saddle system. This will allow greater flexibility for carrying different loads. For more information about availability and price of llama packs, read the annual pack survey issue of *The Backcountry Llama* or the annual packing issue of the *The Llama Link*. The Appendix lists the addresses of these and other llama publications and equipment suppliers.

Before moving on to other necessary equipment, we want to share an idea that will help organize your packs. There is nothing more frustrating than finding, after emptying an entire pannier, that the can opener you were seeking was in the easily accessible side pouch. Attempting to organize your supplies, rather than just throwing them into the pannier, will streamline all camping chores. Our answer to organization? Buckets!

Many restaurants and dining halls buy spaghetti sauce, pickles, and other foods in five-gallon, square, plastic buckets. Two of these buckets will fit into each of our panniers creating four distinct compartments in which to pack supplies. Labels on the lid of each bucket allow us to see in an instant if lunch is in that pack without opening—and even emptying—each one.

In camp, the buckets make convenient seats for tired bodies. Two buckets, wrapped in high density foam, serve as coolers. The bucket's sturdy handles facilitate hauling water and make it easy to hoist food high out of bears' reach. Whether you use plastic buckets or some other system, we strongly recommend that you compartmentalize your panniers.

Brackets make it easy to load panniers onto this soft pack-saddle.

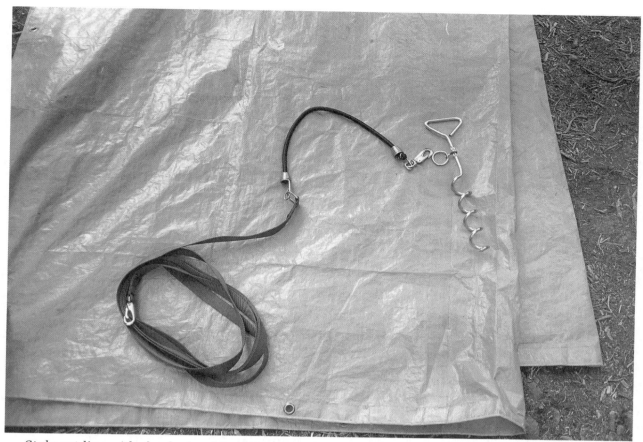

Stakeout line with shock-absorbing bungee cord between corkscrew picket pin and stakeout line.

Additional Equipment

Packs, lead lines, and halters help you move your llamas and supplies along the trail. In camp additional equipment serves to contain and feed your llama. Picket pins, stakeout lines, water and grain containers, a lightweight scale, and grooming and safety equipment round out the list.

Corkscrew picket pins, such as those used for restraining dogs, work well for tethering llamas in camp. The auger part of the pin should be a foot long to provide an ample anchor once screwed into the earth. Corkscrew picket pins leave scarcely a trace after you pull them up, are lightweight, and are easy to use. Pins carved from material found on the trail should not be used as they significantly disturb the soil when pulled up.

Longer stakeout lines replace lead lines once you reach camp. This allows your llama to graze in a larger area than he could if he were secured by a short lead line. The longer stakeout line allows more grazing for your llama with less overgrazing damage to the land. Once your llama has had an opportunity to practice at home on the long stakeout line, he will be able to handle a 25-foot line without getting tangled. One-inch nylon webbing or three-eighths-inch lightweight nylon rope make a light and strong stakeout line. The "Herd Management in the Backcountry" section of In Camp (chapter 9)

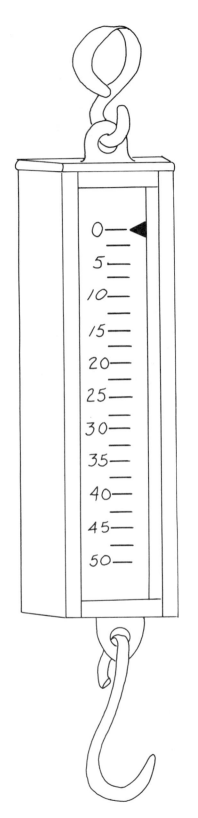

A hand-held load scale will help you balance packs.

provides a more complete discussion of staking.

In camp you will need to water and feed your llamas. Any container that holds two quarts of water and has at least a six-inch diameter opening will work for both tasks. The bottom half of a one gallon plastic milk container is lightweight, durable, waterproof, readily available, and inexpensive. These pliable containers can nest inside each other, reducing the volume in your packs.

Until you are able to estimate weights, we recommend bringing along a hand-held spring scale for weighing and balancing loads. Most llama suppliers sell a lightweight 50-pound-capacity scale that works well.

If you will be packing in bear country, a bell attached to your llama's halter will help alert bears to your presence. However, you should also sing or talk to reduce your chances of a surprise encounter with a bruin. On extended trips where your llama's wool might accumulate debris, a brush will help you groom the area where the saddle will go. Carry the brush in case you need it, but do not feel obligated to use it. It is often better to pick off pine needles and other debris by hand than to get the llama all worked up by brushing.

The equipment mentioned in this chapter will provide you the basics for packing with llamas. With the llamas carrying the load, you have the option of packing mountains of gear into the backcountry. Take what you need—but do not equip yourself out of a good time.

– 7 –

PRE-TRIP PLANNING

Once you have selected, trained, and conditioned your llama and purchased the proper equipment, it's time for a little pre-trip planning before heading out. Where are you going and for how long? What should you expect—and be prepared for—along that route? What should you bring for your llamas and yourself? Based on these decisions, you can best prepare for your needs and the needs of your llamas.

Route Selection

Planning your route before you go will help prevent problems along the trail. Consider the distance to the trailhead, the terrain and distances along the trail, and the weather you might expect.

Your first consideration when selecting a backcountry route is the distance to the trailhead. If the road is long and bumpy, your llama will use up as much energy keeping his balance in the trailer as he would if he had packed a full load for that much time. The rougher the road, the more energy your llamas will use en route and the less they will have for packing.

The distance a llama can travel depends on the topography, weather, weight of the load, pace, and the llama's condition and experience. An experienced, well-conditioned pack llama will be able to carry a full load 15 miles a day through most conditions.

As you sit down with a map to plan your itinerary, you may wonder where you can expect your llama to travel and how far your fully loaded llama will travel in one day. Unfortunately there are no exact answers. The general rule is that the llama can go anywhere his leader can go without the use of hands. If you need to use your hands to scramble up or down an incline, do not expect your fully loaded llama to follow you.

Traversing boulder fields or rock slides requires caution. The rocks themselves pose less of a hazard than the spaces between them. If your llama's feet have been properly conditioned, sharp, jagged rocks—even lava fields—

Be sure to review the map before heading into the backcountry.

should not cut their pads. However, the larger the rocks, the larger the spaces between them, the greater the chance the llama will wedge his foot there—possibly breaking his leg. Fortunately, llamas are very agile and surefooted and can negotiate most boulder fields. Be sure to allow extra time when planning a trip that traverses many boulder fields.

Exercise caution when crossing large rivers with llamas. Llamas can swim, but the combination of fast-moving water and uncertain footing presents problems. A fully loaded llama could lose his footing in a swift current and be swept downstream. A llama will have difficulty crossing a river that is more than chest deep, so plan your route accordingly. However, they can cross slow-moving, belly-deep creeks without much trouble. If you have trouble keeping your balance, your llama will also have problems. If you must cross a strong current, take the panniers off the llama and carry the panniers across yourself. In swift water, the first person in your party to ford the stream or river can string a rope across that the other hikers can hold on to as they cross. You can hook the panniers onto the rope to protect them from being swept downstream if you lose your footing.

If you are heading into the mountains, you might also encounter snow on your trip. The llama's foot, although large, does not provide enough surface area to keep the animals on top of the snow. A certain amount of lunging through the snow is normal, but snow deeper than two feet can pose problems for the pack llama. You should be careful not to ask too much of your llama in these situations. Wading through deep snow is extremely fatiguing and could set the llama up for hypothermia.

In 1979, managers of Sequoia-Kings Canyon National Park took a 110-mile llama trek which included two climbs totaling 5,000 feet. The fully loaded llamas covered an average of 26 miles per day. As a general rule, llamas will cover as much ground as the average hiker carrying a loaded backpack would cover. The pace of the llama is compatible with the human stride, but you should plan extra time to cover any distance. It takes longer to break camp, load

A llama can go anywhere you can go without using your hands.

the panniers, feed and water the llamas, and strap on the packs than to load your gear into a backpack. Llamas also take time along the trail to nibble trailside shrubs and to defecate. (Our summer trekking guests are always surprised and impressed when they see the llamas step neatly off the trail to relieve themselves.)

Cold temperatures do not affect llamas as much as very hot temperatures. On one hunting trip, we camped at 7,500 feet above sea level in one-and-a-half feet of snow. Temperatures dropped to 10 degrees Fahrenheit in the middle of the night and climbed to only 20 degrees the next day as we hiked out. Black-Eyed-Jack, our least woolly llama, shivered a bit early in the morning, but warmed up quickly. In such cold temperatures, plan on taking twice the normal amount of grain to give your llamas the energy to keep warm.

When temperatures reach 95 degrees Fahrenheit, you must take care not to overheat your working llama. Load your llama more lightly and plan on taking frequent breaks. You might also consider shearing your llama (see Care and Feeding, chapter three). Starting early in the morning and quitting by mid-afternoon makes sense on very hot days.

A fully loaded llama can carry 80 pounds of food and gear—enough for one to two people for three to five days.

What to Bring—For Your Llama and Yourself

Now that you know where you are going and for how long, you can figure out what to bring—for both you and your llama. If you own several llamas you will need to decide which to bring and which to leave home. Depending on their personalities, leaving one llama home alone may not be a good idea. He may be so bonded to his pasture mates that he will escape to be with them. You might save yourself some hassle by taking all your llamas, even if some do not carry packs.

Similarly, it is not a good idea to take just one llama and leave the rest at home. Being such social animals, llamas will spend the entire trip humming for their friends back home. However, you will occasionally find a llama who does not mind going off on his own.

Although llamas will meet their nutritional requirements with what grows along the trail in most areas, we carry one pound of corn per llama for each day on the trail. Any high protein grain will work, but a corn/barley mixture provides the best nutrition for the price. A corn/oats/barley mixture with molasses (often called three-way) also works. Besides supplying protein, the grain acts as a reward for their effort and comes in handy for luring a stray llama back to camp.

In the deserts of the Southwest and on snow-covered trails, llamas require additional roughage as well as a protein supplement. We have had good luck with a one-quarter-inch-diameter alfalfa pellet; llamas have difficulty chewing the larger pellets designed for horses. One pound of alfalfa pellets per llama per day will provide sufficient bulk roughage in these sparsely-vegetated environments.

Unless you pack in all the llamas's feed and water, you will need to consider their nutritional needs in your itinerary. Llamas will eat little during the day while they are working, so camp should offer plenty of feed. A grassy meadow would be ideal for grazing the llamas. They will also need water twice a day. Often the animals drink nothing the first day on the trail—maybe because of the excitement of being in new surroundings—but you should offer them water in the morning and evening, whether or not they drink it. Although llamas prefer clean water, they will drink from a bog or mud puddle if thirsty enough. If you will not have access to water on a trip, the llamas will have to carry it for both you and themselves. Anticipating water needs is an important aspect of pre-trip planning.

Based on our experience, a llama drinks about a gallon a day on the trail. This may vary with each individual llama, the amount of energy used that day, the water content of the grasses nibbled, and the weather. However, do not make the mistake of thinking that just because llamas and camels are members of the same family, llamas can match camels in conserving water.

With the feed and water out of the way, you can assemble the other necessary llama gear we discussed in chapter six. The Appendix includes a checklist of items we take with us on our commercial llama pack trips. Pay close attention to the gear listed on the "Llama Gear Checklist," as the welfare of your llama may depend upon you having these supplies. We will help you assemble a llama first aid kit—mandatory equipment!—in chapter ten. The rest of the items are more a matter of personal preference, but modifying our list is probably easier than starting from scratch.

Once you have outfitted your llama, you can gather your own gear for the trip. Many fine books on camping and camping equipment

Keeping your gear organized at home will make it easy to gather equipment for a trip. Top photo: Picket pins, bungees, and scale. Bottom photo: Saddles, saddle blankets, cinches, and panniers.

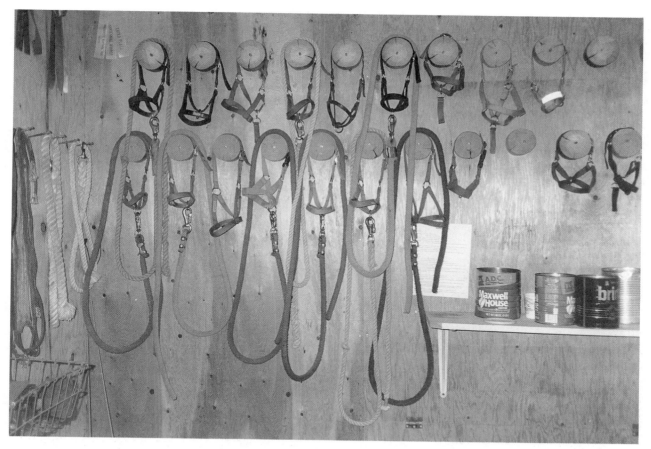

Each llama should have his own halter for the trail, fitted with plenty of room for chewing.

exist that will help you with this task. The following brief overview will help you start gathering clothing, equipment, and supplies.

The season and location will dictate your choice of clothing. At high elevations, where temperatures can be cool even in midsummer, it's best to dress in layers of clothing rather than one large jacket or one heavy pair of pants. The layers trap air next to your body, insulating you while allowing you to regulate your body temperature by adding or removing one layer at a time. For example, if you have long underwear, a wool sweater, and a raincoat/windbreaker, you are set for a much wider range of temperatures and weather conditions than if you simply bring a heavy down parka. Much of your body heat escapes through your head, so be sure to pack a warm hat (wool or pile), especially if you plan to sleep under the stars.

If there is any chance of rain, pack rain gear. Even a warm rain, especially if accompanied by a breeze, will chill you or even make you hypothermic. Rain pants are handy in the morning when the grass is wet with dew. We also suggest carrying an extra pair of lightweight footwear and several pairs of socks. Tennis shoes are a nice change around camp and leave a lighter track than heavy, lug-soled hiking boots. Warm socks can double as mittens if the weather turns cold. Nothing feels more luxurious when you get into camp at night than taking off wet hiking boots, and putting on warm, dry socks and tennis shoes.

For hot, dry climates and high elevations, be sure to pack clothing to protect you from the sun's harmful rays. Wide brimmed hats, light-colored clothing, sunglasses, lip balm, and sunscreen are essential.

Check the contents of your kitchen boxes against your list to make sure you bring everything you need.

Packing with llamas gives you the option to bring a lot of clothes. Take what you need to be comfortable in a variety of conditions, but don't overdo it. Four pairs of jeans for a five day trip are too much.

While the Appendix lists the essential equipment for a llama pack trip, a few items, such as those for waste disposal, water purification, and treating emergencies, call for some explanation.

Failure to carry out trash or properly dispose of human waste will ruin the campsite for those who come after you. Bears can become accustomed to eating garbage, which inevitably leads to problems with human-bear encounters and death of the bear. Also, human waste from a latrine placed too close to water can contaminate streams and lakes.

The best way to dispose of human waste (feces) in the backcountry is to dig a small cat hole or latrine and bury it. Pick a spot for your latrine that is away from camp, water, and trails. The organisms necessary to decompose human feces are near the surface, so don't make your hole too deep. Six inches is deep enough. Pack a small trowel or collapsible shovel to dig the hole. Either burn the used toilet paper in the cat hole or back at your campfire, or pack it out, otherwise animals will dig it up and eat it. Bring along some extra plastic bags for packing out the used toilet paper. We hang one plastic bag on the tree at the site of the latrine and at the end of our stay in that camp we remove the bag. This is a handy way for women to dispose of tampons in camp as well. When we are packing with a group, we dig a two-foot-long, six-inch-deep trench to serve as the latrine. After using the latrine, the person simply fills it in at one end of the hole. This method of a group latrine results in less soil disturbance, as everyone isn't out digging his or her own private latrine.

Water in the western United States and parts of Canada and Mexico, even in the most remote areas, has been infected with a microscopic, single-celled parasite called *Giardia*. *Giardia* is a microscopic animal that lives in the water until ingested by a host, whereupon it attaches itself to the digestive tract where it lives and reproduces. It is then carried in feces from humans and other animals. After an incubation period of several weeks, the host suffers from nausea, persistent diarrhea, severe stomach cramps, and, if not treated, can become quite ill. The problem with *Giardia* has become more and more widespread through human careless-

ness, until it is not safe to drink the water in even the remotest wilderness. There are three ways to protect yourself from *Giardia*: filtering, boiling, or chemically treating the water. All three methods have advantages and disadvantages and you will need to decide which is best for you.

Chemical treatment consists of placing a small purifying pill in the container of water, shaking it to mix, and waiting the full amount of time indicated on the package instructions. These pills are convenient and lightweight but give the water a chemical taste. The pills are available in sporting goods stores. Boiling the water only requires a pot and enough fuel to keep the water boiling for twenty minutes. If you want good tasting, hassle-free water, a lightweight hand-held water filter is best. However, plan on spending $50 or more to get one

Filtering drinking water to remove Giardia. *We haul a bucket of water to camp and attach the filter to the lid of the bucket for easy pumping.*

with a fine enough filter to block the very small *Giardia* protozoa. Check the label to be sure it will filter out *Giardia*.

Soapy water can also pollute the backcountry if allowed to contaminate lakes and streams. Plan ahead and purchase biodegradable, phosphate-free dish soap and hand soap at your local camping supply store or via mail order. Dip water out of the stream for use in bathing and rinse off all soap well away from the water. That way you will not risk contaminating the water. Dump soapy dishwater 200 feet or more from the edge of the water. Bathing without soap is really the best option, but if you feel that you must use some cleanser in the backcountry, try to use it sparingly, and consider non-soap alter-

natives such as horsetail cleanser or castille "soap". These are usually available at natural food stores.

Backcountry weather conditions can change quickly. Being caught unprepared is a potentially dangerous situation. You will be far from professional medical assistance and must anticipate a variety of emergencies. Your emergency supplies should include matches or a lighter, paper, and even some kindling to get a fire started for warmth; a space blanket to help you retain body warmth; a whistle to blow should you become lost; compass and maps (and the knowledge to use them); and a human first-aid kit.

Billy the Kid carries a cross-cut saw arched across the top of his panniers.

This soft packsaddle allows versatility in packing your load with room on top for sleeping bags or tents. Julio carries a fishing pole case on one side.

Packing Up

Before departing for the trailhead, you need to load and balance the panniers. Packing up at home, before departure, is convenient and shortens the llama's anxious wait at the trailhead.

Make a plan before you start stuffing gear and supplies into the packs. For easy access, supplies that will be needed first should go into the pannier last. Sharp objects should be placed where they will not poke or irritate the llama's ribs. Sleeping bags, sleeping pads, and tents can ride on top of the saddle if your panniers have straps to attach a top load. Bulky, awkward items, such as an axe, saw, and shovel, can also be fastened to the packsaddle. This will save digging into a pack each time a tree must be cleared off the trail or someone needs to relieve himself. However, do not put anything too heavy on top where it will press directly on the llama's spine. Also be careful that top loads, such as tent poles or other hard objects, do not press against the llama's back or neck.

On the last llama in line, we pack gear inside the panniers only (no top load). A top load can shift and fall off a llama without anyone notic-

Weighing panniers. Balance panniers to within three pounds.

ing. On a recent trip, a brand new tent stuffed in a green bag slipped out of the top straps and fell off King after he jumped across a log. Two members of our group hiked past the tent before the last person in line happened to spot it in the bushes alongside the trail. If top-loaded gear falls off the last llama, you might not miss it until you arrive in camp for the night.

The two panniers in a pair should balance each other. An inexpensive load scale and a little patience is all that is needed for the job. A difference in pannier weight of more than three pounds might cause the load to shift on the llama. Continually stopping to readjust the pack is frustrating and time consuming—and relatively easy to prevent.

Horse and mule packers have a rule for distributing the weight of the load in each pannier that also applies to llamas: the load's center of gravity should lie one-third of the way below the top of the pannier, centered between the llama's side and the outside of the pack. Top- or bottom-heavy loads sway from side to side, and the llama will waste energy keeping his balance. You may never get the weight distributed perfectly, but by placing the heavier objects near the center of the pannier, you will eliminate most sway.

Pre-trip planning, an essential part of the outing, can be a lot of fun. Poring over maps, selecting destinations, and imagining the scenery add to the excitement of the outing. Preparing yourself with reasonable loads, sensible clothing and gear, and the proper skills and equipment for emergencies ensures that your pack trip will meet all your expectations.

– 8 –

HITTING THE TRAIL

After much preparation, it's finally time to pack 'em up and head 'em out. Unless you live next to the area you plan to explore, you will need to load your llamas into a trailer or vehicle and drive to the trailhead. In this chapter, we explain how to safely transport your stock, load up, and hit the trail. We emphasize planning, trail etiquette, and safety and offer tips for catching a runaway llama.

Getting There: Choosing Your Transportation

Llamas are very agile and can ride in a wide variety of vehicles. Vans, trucks, and trailers are most commonly used to transport llamas, but about any vehicle the llama can fit into comfortably will work. We have a friend with an older model, four-door Volvo. For short trips, he removes the back seat and loads his pack llama, Woody, through the back door. We headed home after our local fair one year, following the Volvo down the highway. We enjoyed many good laughs watching the reactions as the Volvo passed other cars—Woody's head sticking out the rear window.

For hauling one, two, or three llamas, the bed of a standard-size pickup truck works nicely. Smaller trucks can carry two small llamas. Your truck should have a stock rack to keep the llamas from jumping out of the truck. Awnings are also available that stretch across the top of a stock rack to provide a covered enclosure. A friend of ours watched in horror as her llama jumped up over the standard stock rack and exited the back of her new pick-up truck. The llama did a sort of somersault but landed without injury. Our friend added an extension to the stock rack and now carefully ties her llama on a short lead when he is in the truck.

Many llama owners transport their pack animals in a pickup with a topper or cap over the bed, forcing the llamas to lie down. These folks begin training their young llamas to load into the pickup truck. As the llamas grow, the owners continue this training until the adults actually learn to crawl in on their knees. If you have

McGruder weighs over 400 pounds but still rides comfortably in this small pickup. Side extensions allow plenty of headroom under the cap.

trouble getting your llamas to crawl under your topper, consider jacking it up with a side extension.

Vans work well for hauling up to three llamas. Sharing the cab of your van with a llama is a special experience. Your sense of fellowship begins as you depart for the trailhead. With the llama inside the van, you can better monitor his mood and health throughout the ride. Unfortunately, on long trips you also will be the first to know when the llama defecates. Lining the floor of the van with a scrap piece of carpet helps absorb urine and provides a non-slip surface for the llama. After the trip you can pull the carpet out for cleaning.

Many people haul llamas in a trailer towed behind a vehicle. Horse trailers work well but,

designed to carry 1,200-pound horses, are heavier than you need. If you have a horse trailer, use it. Otherwise consider buying a lightweight utility trailer that can be hauled with a smaller, more energy-efficient vehicle.

What size trailer do you need for hauling more than one llama? We use a six-by-twelve-foot utility trailer to haul seven llamas comfortably. Last year, we moved our entire herd to a new location. We had no trouble fitting all seventeen llamas into a 24-foot trailer, and they had room to spare in their four separate compartments. You can fit three llamas in a two-horse trailer if you take out the middle divider. Six or seven llamas will fit in a four-horse trailer depending on the size of the llamas and the configuration of the trailer.

After only one training session with the van backed up to a hill, Zip has learned to pick up his feet without hitting the bumper, and now rides calmly in the van.

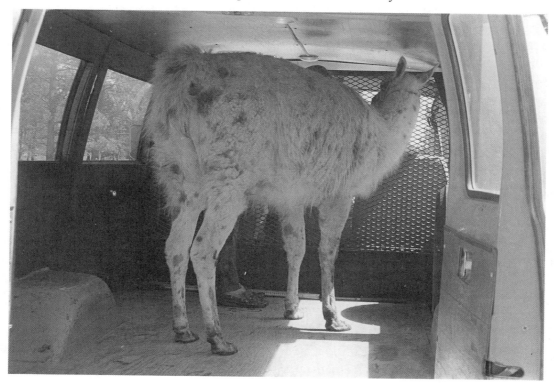

What you use for a tow vehicle depends on the weight of your load. Every vehicle is rated for how much it can safely tow. Make sure your tow vehicle matches the load and type of trailer it will be pulling. A small, four-cylinder pickup truck, for instance, will be greatly strained towing a four-horse trailer and a ton of llamas. If your trailer is too heavy for your towing vehicle, you will have trouble climbing hills, steering, and braking.

Remember as well that the air we drive through is full of bugs. Colliding with a bug at sixty miles-per-hour, especially if it lands in an eye, can cause pain and injury. If you are using a stock rack on a pickup or have an open trailer, mount a sheet of plywood or some other deflector across the front of the stock rack to protect the llamas' eyes from bugs.

Loading Up

When you are ready to go, load the full panniers and the rest of the equipment into your vehicle first. Then load the llamas. This reduces the time the llamas spend in the strange environment of the trailer or vehicle.

You can transport the llamas with their saddles on. We do this and it speeds up the process of loading them up at the trailhead. However, we advise against trailering saddled if you use sawbuck saddles—they could hook into and injure another llama in the trailer.

If you are using a horse trailer, your llama will be able to step in easily. Loading into a pickup or van requires a bit more training. One of the problems you will encounter is that the llama will unwittingly step too close to the vehicle to lift his front legs, and he will bang his knees on the bumper. You can teach the llama to raise his front legs before he gets to the vehicle by placing an object, such as a bale of hay, on the ground and leaning it against the bumper. To avoid hitting the obstacle, the llama will have to start his jump a foot before he reaches the bumper. After just a few loadings, your llama will get the idea and should jump into the van or pickup unassisted by props.

Once you have the llama in the trailer or vehicle you need to decide whether to tie him or to let him ride untied. If you will be loading more llamas in the same space you will probably need to tie the first llama—at least until all the llamas are loaded. Before we depart, we unclip the llamas' lead lines and leave the animals free to move about the trailer. An untied llama is unlikely to accidentally strangle himself or slip and break his neck en route to the trailhead. Occasionally, we need to tie one or two llamas to keep them from fighting. If they are going to ride standing, tie them with a foot or less lead between the head and the knot. The llama tied this way will not be able to lie down. If you want your llama to lie down, say in the back of a pickup, tie his head low (two feet off the ground) with one foot of lead between the head and the knot. This will urge the llama to ride lying down. If untied llamas have enough room, they almost always lie down once underway and remain down for the duration of the ride. The low profile provides extra stability and keeps the llamas from being tossed around when you hit the brakes or round a corner.

To secure the llama in the trailer or on the trail, use a quick-release knot that allows you to untie the llama in a hurry. (The Appendix provides instructions on how to tie a good quick-release knot.) This knot works well whether tied to a tree, a log, or the support on a trailer. Learn this knot and use it.

When we load seven llamas into our trailer, we tie them with their heads facing the sides of the trailer (instead of facing forward). We can put more llamas in the trailer this way, and they take the bumps better loaded sideways. We also alternate the direction each llama faces, ending up with a head next to a tail next to a head, and so on. This leaves a llama's body width between heads and prevents spitting between llamas. After all the llamas are loaded we reach in from outside the trailer and unhook their leads.

As soon as you have the llamas loaded, get rolling. Once underway, the llamas will concentrate on balancing themselves and forget about spitting at each other.

Gallatin started loading into this mid-sized pickup as a youngster and still manages to fit in as an adult.

With the truck backed up to a slight slope, Gallatin can enter the truck without jumping.

Gallatin moves to the front of the truck bed on his knees in the kush position. His lead is tied, leaving room for him to sightsee enroute to the trailhead.

A nimble llama: Gallatin manages to turn around on his knees and unload without bumping his head or back.

Keeping It Safe

Just because llamas transport easily is no reason to take the matter lightly. You are speeding down the highway with their health in your hands. Car accidents are serious for buckled-in humans and even more so for unrestrained llamas. Minor scrapes or bumps can send your llama flying. A human's broken leg can be repaired; a pack llama's broken leg may mean the end for that animal. When hauling llamas, your driving habits must compensate for the extra weight in live cargo.

Suppose your import pickup truck is pulling a utility trailer carrying two llamas. Suddenly, the vehicle that usually stops only its own weight must stop an additional one-and-a-half tons. Unless you anticipate stops and curves and start braking much sooner, you will be pushed by the weight of the trailer and llamas through an intersection or off a curve. Trailer brakes reduce the amount of push on the tow vehicle, and we highly recommend them, especially if you will be hauling more than two llamas. Even with trailer brakes, you will need to compensate for the additional weight by anticipating slowdowns, stops, and hazards.

Llamas will often lie down when transported, especially for their first few trips, but if one or more llamas in the trailer might spit or kick, the others will ride standing. If one of your llamas is standing, take extra care when driving. Braking and accelerating gradually and taking curves slowly will allow the llama to keep his balance. The less energy the llama uses in the trailer, the more energy he will have for the trail.

On your way to the trailhead think for a few moments of why you are going there. If you are like most people, you are seeking solitude, beautiful scenery, and recreational opportunities. Strangely enough, the moment you arrive you negatively impact the very qualities you seek. Everywhere we go, we leave clues of our passage. As people grow to respect and love our wild lands, they want to spend time in the wilderness. As more people venture into the wilderness, our lands become less wild.

But it does not have to be this way. Camping techniques can minimize the traces we leave behind. They take a little extra effort, but if you care about our wild lands you will do your best to reduce your impact. Developing a personal wilderness ethic will help guide you toward proper decisions in the backcountry.

Backcountry Bound

Whether you reach the trailhead in a pickup, van, or stock trailer, unloading your llamas should be your first priority. Once they are out, you can strap on the saddles, attach the panniers, and start hiking.

The llamas will feel most comfortable walking head first out of the trailer or vehicle. Llamas that do not have room to pivot inside the trailer can back out if they have been trained to do so. Unload all the llamas and tie them to some support. The sooner they get outside, the sooner they will find their walking legs again. Using a quick-release knot, tie each llama on a short lead to a secure anchor at the llama's head height. Allow less than one foot between the llama's head and the tie-off point. This way, he will not be able to sidestep when you try to put on the pack.

Since you packed the panniers before departing for the trailhead, simply strap on the saddles and attach the already balanced panniers. Put saddles on all the llamas before attaching any

Unload your llama using a short lead so the animal can't jump.

panniers so no animal has to stand around loaded while you are working on the others. If you trailer with saddles on the llamas, you need only to quickly check and possibly tighten the cinches before putting on the panniers. The cinches should fit snugly, but allow room to slide two fingers between the cinch and the llama's belly. Back cinches do not need to be as tight as front cinches, but both tend to loosen as they settle into the wool. If you will be starting out traveling uphill, tighten up the breast strap; if downhill, tighten up the breeching or crupper.

With the animals loaded, car lights off, and doors locked, you are ready to hit the trail. Leave an extra set of keys at the vehicle in case of an emergency, and tell members of your party

where you hid them. Now, pull the end of the quick release knot and start up the trail.

Walk with the lead looped in the palm of your hand—not wrapped around it. If the llama bolts and you have the lead line wrapped around your hand, you could suffer a severe rope burn or even be dragged down the trail.

Start out with each person leading one llama, at least until the animals get over their initial excitement of being on the trail. If you have more than one llama, you will need to decide which one goes first and who follows whom. Some llamas will hate to be followed by another and will jockey for the tail position. Others are only happy if they are next to their best buddy or leading the pack. Try the llamas in different positions and see which configuration works

How to load up a sawbuck (six photos). A. Check for burrs, sticks, and debris in the saddle area before putting on the saddle blanket.

B. Place the saddle in the center of the back, then adjust the sawbuck to fit the llama.

C. The front cinch should cross the abdomen just behind the front legs.

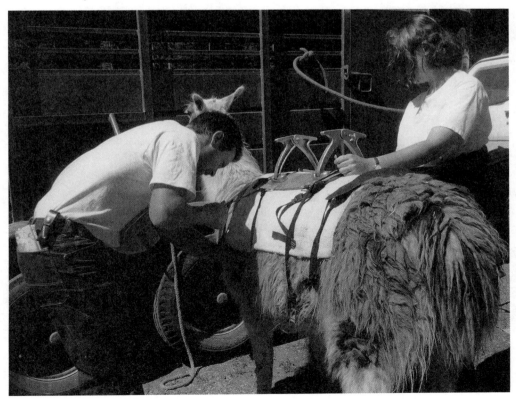

D. Fasten the breast strap and breeching strap. The breeching will ride six to eight inches lower once the llama starts walking and the rigging settles into the wool.

E. and F. Load both sides to keep the saddle centered.

best. Knowing how your llamas interact before you go packing will simplify this process.

After hiking just a short while, the llamas will probably try to nip a little snack. Eating along the trail is acceptable for llamas as long as you decide when it is snack time. If you let the llamas decide, you will spend the day in the nearest meadow. Keep them moving, and when you stop for a break, let the llamas eat. They will have plenty of time to eat once you get to camp.

A few tugs keep the llamas from snacking. When they are defecating however, you will need to stop. Unlike horses, which defecate while walking, llamas need to stop to take care of their business. The first thing we look for when we feel a llama resisting is whether he needs to relieve himself. The tell-tale signs are walking off the trail and attempting to spread his hind legs. If you see this, stop and be patient. Encouraging all the llamas to go at once will save time. Allow the other llamas to smell the feces and urine. This will give them the urge to defecate too.

After hiking five or ten minutes, the llamas will probably be over any high spirits, and you can tie several together as a pack string if you choose. The same quick-release knot used to tie your llama also works best to string llamas together (See Appendix). Tie the lead of one llama to the rear of the saddle of the llama in front of it. We attach a pigtail—a loop of leather or other easily breakable material—as the con-

Allow your llamas to graze when you stop for a break—not while you are hiking.

nection between the lead line of one animal and the saddle of the other. If one of the llamas falls off a cliff or spooks, the pigtail will break instead of pulling the other llamas along. Although llamas are generally calm animals that rarely spook, one panicked llama can deliver a long pack string into a tangled mess in a hurry. For this reason, keep your string small when possible. Three animals are manageable, but we sometimes string as many as five experienced llamas together.

Whether you are leading one llama or a string, try to keep the stock in the middle of an established trail, as the edges are sensitive to trampling. If a lone llama starts walking to your side, swing the loose end of the lead in a circle to urge him back in line. If one llama in a string walks on the side of the trail, move him to the front of the string where you can more easily control his position.

Single llamas generally follow the leader. When leading a string of llamas, remember to slow down through any curve until the last llama has rounded the bend. This will keep him from being jerked through the turn, shortcutting the switchback. Taking shortcuts across

Leather thong forms a break-away "pigtail" between saddle and carabiner. Tie leadline using quick-release knot. In an emergency you can quickly release the knot and slide the leadline out of the carabiner.

switchbacks might save you a few steps but will soon create a multiple-lane, eroded trail. Resist the temptation to cut switchbacks, and stay on the trail.

A washed-out bridge, a landslide, or other hazard may necessitate going cross-country. If this situation should arise, you will need to reverse your thinking about how to minimize impacts. If you are traveling with a group of people, spread out rather than follow the same route. This will lessen the chance of establishing a new trail. When possible, travel on durable, non-vegetated surfaces such as bare rock, sand, gravel, snow, and ice. Avoid wet soils or steep slopes, and do not cut blazes on trees or you will certainly create a new trail.

After the first hour of walking, the llamas will be ready for a break. Find a spot where you can get off the trail where there is feed for the llamas and tie each animal to a tree or shrub. During a short break, the llamas will not damage the tree or the surrounding area. For breaks lasting less than an hour, it is not necessary to remove the llamas' loads. They can lie down and get up fully loaded. If you are going to break for more than an hour, consider removing the llamas' panniers and leaving the saddles attached. It does not take much effort to remove the panniers, and the llamas will appreciate it.

If your llama decides to take a break before you do, he will lie down on the trail. Llamas are experts in passive resistance. A mature, well-

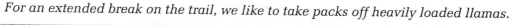

For an extended break on the trail, we like to take packs off heavily loaded llamas.

conditioned pack llama will likely never do this. However, expect the younger members of your pack string to attempt (at least once) to lie down at a strenuous uphill or downhill section of trail or at the end of the day. A llama may also try to lie down if his packsaddle rigging has shifted to an uncomfortable position. A tight rear crupper, a cinch across the penis sheath, or a breast strap chaffing between the front legs may cause your llama to try to lie down. First, get your llama up quickly. Then, walk a short distance and give him a break. That way you will be the one who decides when to take a break. Check and adjust the pack once your llama is resting.

Rushing at your llama shouting and clapping your hands will startle him up if he is just starting to lie down. The person behind you on the trail will be in a better position to see when your llama is starting to lie down and can startle him from behind while you pull on the lead. To raise your llama once he is firmly seated, you may need to slide your hand between his back legs until you are touching his sensitive belly and penis sheath, or push him to one side so that he feels slightly off-center and at risk of rolling onto his side. One of these techniques usually will work. If not, you need to determine if your llama has more than an attitude problem and needs first aid for heat stress or muscle exhaustion. See the First Aid (chapter ten) for more information on these problems.

Tough Spots

Although we visit the backcountry to get away from people, more than likely we will bump into someone on the trail. Llama owners, being the new guys on the block, have a special obligation to learn the rules of social conduct in the backcountry. Getting through tough spots, such as chance meetings and natural obstacles, without incident is one of the keys to a successful trip.

When you and your llama meet another group on the trail, you must decide who is most able to get off the trail to let the other pass. Hikers can get off the trail more easily than llamas and should be asked to move to the downhill side of the trail while you pass. Realize, however, the hiker may want to stop and visit with your woolly companion before passing. Many people hike with their dogs. If you meet a hiker with a dog ask if he or she could restrain the dog until you pass. If the owner cannot get control of the dog, but you do not think the dog will bite, position yourself between the dog and the llama and try to pass.

Take special care when meeting horses or mules on the trail. If the horse or mule is "green" or has never seen a llama before, the horse or mule might spook. This is dangerous for the horse rider and could spell disaster for a pack string of horses or mules. We cannot stress enough the importance of having smooth, non-confrontational encounters with other stock. Many stockmen in the western United States and Canada still view the llama as an exotic creature that should not be allowed on trails. In fact, Lewis and Clark National Forest in Montana actually closed certain trails to llama use in 1989. The ruling was overturned, but the fact remains: llamas are not welcomed by all. Our summer outfitting trips usually take us into the Lolo National Forest; however we take one trip along a trail into the Bob Marshall Wilderness that horse outfitters use heavily. In the first five

Lonnie and Billy, two members of our pack string, spent time visiting the Forest Service pack stock so the horses and mules could become accustomed to llamas before meeting them on the trail. The horses and mules had to pass the llama pen to get to water.

Although many people believe mules will never get along with llamas, our llamas have had no problems sharing a very large pasture with horses and mules after first becoming accustomed to one another across the fence.

miles of trail we pass over one hundred head of horses and mules. These animals are well-trained pack stock, and they completely ignore our llamas.

Surprise meetings between horses and llamas have the most potential for problems. Be especially cautious when approaching blind curves or rises in the trail. If some hikers in your party are not leading a llama, have them scout the trail ahead to warn you for approaching horses. If you are alone, stop and listen before entering the blind curve or peak. Should you hear horses coming, tie your animal and walk ahead to warn the party that there are llamas on the trail. If the riders aren't familiar with llamas, explain that horses will sometimes spook if they have never seen a llama.

After making verbal contact with the approaching riders, move your llama to the down-hill side of the trail. Should a horse spook, a rider can more easily control the animal when it is running uphill. Take your llamas at least fifty yards off the trail and stand still. The llamas may get a bit restive but will not become terribly upset, even if it is their first encounter with horses. If the slope drops off too steeply below the trail, turn the llamas around and hike back to a stretch where the horses can pass safely. The last thing we want is to cause a disaster and have someone get hurt. For the safety of the rider and the benefit of other llama packers, do whatever it takes to make the encounter a pleasant one.

We have made concerted effort in our area to give the Forest Service horses and mules an opportunity to become familiar with llamas. One spring, we put two of our llamas into a small corral in a large pasture with several hundred head of horses and mules. These animals had to pass the llama pen to get to their water. Within a week, the novelty of the new neighbors had worn off, and the horses passed the llama pen without concern. Although meeting llamas on the trail might still be a new experience for the people on summer trail crews, it will not be for their stock animals.

Many horse and mule owners swear something innately different about the smell or appearance of a llama will automatically spook every horse. Some of these people also claim that mules will never tolerate llamas. We have found this to be false. One summer we pastured some of our llamas with a group of horses and mules on forty-acres of hillside. By coincidence, a shortage of stalls at the county fair later that summer landed these same mules in the llama barn. Imagine people's surprise when they saw these mules calmly sharing the barn with llamas. Little did they know that these barnmates had already spent several months together at home. After the fair, our male herd pastured across a flimsy two-strand electric fence from these same horses and mules—without incident.

We once brought our llamas to a meeting of the local Backcountry Horsemen Association. The "green" horses at the meeting were frightened of the llamas—and about anything else that came anywhere near the green horses' corner of the equestrian park. In contrast, the seasoned trail horses showed moderate curiosity but no inclination to spook at either the llamas, bicycles, baby strollers, balloons, or running kids.

In addition to making the best of human and horse encounters, you must be able to surmount natural obstacles. The smart llama packer will prepare for these situations before entering the backcountry. Downed trees and bridges can easily be simulated around the farm. Training and Conditioning (chapter five) explains how to train for these obstacles.

Crossing rushing water, which is not so easy to simulate at home, may pose some problems. At first, your llama may decide to jump the stream rather than walk through it. Llamas cannot jump without first throwing their head up to lift their front legs off the ground. To

Keep your llama moving across the stream.

prevent this, hold the llama's head low, at the level of his chest, and make him walk through the water. Once the llama has started across the stream, keep him moving. If you want to let him drink, do so while he is still standing on the bank, before entering the stream. Something about the rushing water gives llamas the urge to defecate. Do not allow them to relieve themselves in the water. Keep the llama moving until you are at least 200 feet from the other side of the stream, then allow him to defecate if he still wants to.

Most of the wildlife you meet on the trail will tolerate llamas. During the day, when the lla-mas can see there is no threat to them, they will practically ignore deer, elk, and moose. After dark, when they can only half see the animal, they may become frightened and utter a bray-like alarm call until they figure out what they see.

Two animals that deserve special caution when packing with llamas are rattlesnakes and bears. In the southern United States, a few llamas have died from rattlesnake bites. Apparently, curiosity killed the llama. If a llama hears a rattle, he will likely investigate. Upon seeing a snake, the curious llama will lower his head for a closer look. The snake will probably bite

*Bridges such as this one
are not safe for llamas to
cross.*

*This bridge into the
Selway-Bitterroot Wilder-
ness of Idaho was
constructed for pack
stock.*

118

the llama on the nose, causing it to swell until the nostrils shut, suffocating the llama. (See section on snakes in First Aid, chapter ten.)

Llama packers used to think that bears, black and grizzly, were afraid of llamas. Some people picketed a llama in front of their tent at night, expecting the llama to sound a loud alarm call to give advance warning of a nearby bear. However, llamas are vulnerable to bear attacks, as recently proven when a black bear killed two llamas in Colorado. Although bears probably find a llama's appearance and smell strange, that might not be enough to keep the bear at bay. Following normal precautions for hiking in bear country will usually keep you and your party safe in bear country. However, problem bears will attack and kill llamas as quickly as they will cattle, sheep or humans. If you are planning a trip into an area with a known problem of bear-human confrontations, find another place to go packing. The Appendix lists references that provide more information on camping safely in bear country.

Llama On The Loose

At some point in your packing career, you will inevitably wind up with a llama loose on the trail. Do not panic, especially if you have other llamas under your control. Rarely, if ever, will a single llama take off and leave his companions. If you have easy access to grain, offer him some. As he approaches, get on the side of his body that his lead is dragging on. Do not lunge for the dragging lead, but casually step on the end of it and then bend down to pick it up.

The aloof llama may be harder to catch. Look for a physical barrier (fallen log or large boulders) to help corral the animal. If none is available, form a mobile corral by having other members in your party surround the llama holding outstretched arms or a long rope at hip height. Speak quietly and approach the llama slowly and catch him as you would in your corral at home. Once the llama is cornered, he will give in to being caught.

Although many things could go wrong while packing with llamas, problems are rare. If you go equipped with a bit of common sense and a well-trained and conditioned llama, you will be able to handle most situations that arise.

End of the Season Packing Tips

The golden leaves have fallen, and for fair-weather outfitters, the summer packing season is over. Early one spring, we were starting to think we had this llama packing business down to a science. However, not far into the season we realized there was still a thing or two we didn't know. Luckily, we were able to learn a few lessons without hurting any people or llamas. By passing to you the following tips, perhaps you won't have to learn the hard way as we did.

Neck Collar, X-type
Halter Eliminates Abrasions

One July, we did a trek into the Bob Marshall Wilderness Area. We had thirteen clients, so we saddled ten pack llamas for the 44-mile round trip to the Chinese Wall. On day five of the seven day trip, we noticed Black-Eyed-Jack wasn't grazing as the rest of llamas were. On closer inspection, we noticed Jack had rubbed himself raw where the nylon halter crossed his lower jaw bones. The standard extra-large llama halter fit as loose as it could without riding down on the soft part of his nose. We checked other llamas and some of them also had spots where their halter had started to chafe. Jack is calm enough that we knew we could catch him with grain and then remove his halter. This done, Jack started eating and chewing his cud, and we finished the trip without a hitch.

When we got home we had the local saddle maker sew the female end of a Fastex buckle to the end of a two-foot piece of one-inch nylon webbing. The other end we fitted with the male end of the buckle and adjusted it to approxi-

mately the size of a llama neck, creating a neck collar. Then we ordered a few of the X-type nylon halters. The side straps of these X-type halters cross under the lower jaw. This type of halter tightens only when the lead is pulled, remaining loose otherwise, allowing the llama to chew his cud without interference.

The next trip out, we put the X-type halters on the sensitive llamas. When we got to camp, we put the neck collars on the llamas, clipped the stakeout line to the collars, and removed the halters. The llamas haven't had any abrasions since they started wearing the X-type halters and the neck collars.

Standard halter.

Cross-style halter. The noseband crosses under the chin, forming an X, and runs up to the side of the cheek.

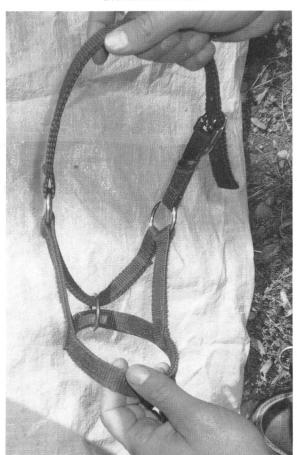

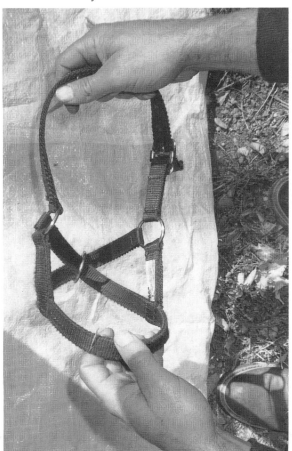

Depending on the shape of your llama's head (the Roman-nosed types seem more susceptible), the toughness of their skin, and the length of your trip, you may do just fine with the standard llama halter. If you have abrasion problems, try the X-type halter and/or the neck collars. Remember to leave enough room for the llama's jaw to run its full figure-eight pattern of chewing. Also, remember the neck collar rides lower on the llama's neck than his halter—giving him more power to pull against his tether. When using neck collars be sure to secure the llama to a sturdy anchor.

Tie Your Llama to a Secure and Sturdy Anchor

One August, we took a trip to the Great Burn Wilderness Area in western Montana. We were feeling a bit relaxed because we had pulled off a couple of incident-free trips since the halter problem. Everything was fine until we stopped for lunch on a saddle above Hidden Lake. Many of the guests were leading llamas, so we instructed them to tie the animals to a tree—we would only be there a half hour and would do no damage to the tree.

Trees were sparse near this lunch spot, so we got the clever idea of tying Billy-the-Kid to Dave's heavily weighted green backpack, which he had dropped on the grassy hillside. Lunch was proceeding peacefully when a loud rustling turned us all from our plates. Next we saw Billy flying past us—with a green backpack in hot pursuit. Down the hill and through some trees he burst at break-neck speed (no pun intended). We thought the backpack would surely snag and break Billy's neck. Finally it did catch, but fortunately his halter snapped, not his neck.

His running had frightened other llamas, and two had loosened their knots and were free. Billy was so worked up that he gave an alarm

Tie your llama to a secure anchor at lunch time.

121

Use a quick release knot to secure your llama when you stop for lunch along the trail. Leave the line long enough to permit your llama to graze.

call and headed back to the trailhead with his buddy King Kong right behind him. We were able to catch the third llama before he could join Billy and King. We kicked our butts as we jogged the three miles back to the trailhead. By the time we got there, Billy and King had calmed enough to let us catch them.

While returning to the lunch spot, we had time to reflect on what had happened. Dave's backpack weighed about thirty pounds. Even though the ground sloped only gently, that was enough for the backpack to start rolling when Billy unwittingly pulled on the attached lead. Once the pack started toward Billy, he jumped away, pulling the backpack even faster toward himself. The faster he ran, the faster the green monster chased him.

Although it may be convenient to tether your llama to your backpack, don't do it! Choose a secure anchor that will hold your llama. Billy was lucky. His halter broke; your llama's halter may not. When tethering overnight, we attach a short piece of rubber tubing or strap to one end of the line to provide elasticity and an emergency breaking point should the llama panic and try to run.

As we put our gear away for the season, we can reflect on four things we learned this year: an X-type halter and a neck collar can help prevent halter sores; never tether a llama to anything but a secure anchor; for overnight, always use a rubber shock-absorber between the llama and the anchor; and, most importantly, we all have things to learn. Share your tips with others so we can all enjoy the backcountry with minimum damage to ourselves, our llamas, and our wildlands.

– 9 –

IN CAMP

A few hours of daylight remain before dark, and your legs tell you it is time to quit the trail and find a campsite. In your mind you have an idea of what makes a good backpacker's camp. A place for a tent, nearby water, protection from the elements, and seclusion are desirable. When camping with pack stock, there is an additional consideration: finding a site at least 200 feet from camp, trails, and water and with ample grass for grazing.

Don't wait until the stars are shining in the evening sky before selecting your site. Allow at least two hours to set up camp and to take care of your woolly companions. Too often people will go just a little farther and find themselves having to use a bad site—bad for themselves, the llamas, and the environment.

Selecting a Campsite

Wherever we camp, we leave signs of our stay. Trampled vegetation, fire rings, and newly worn trails all betray our visit. The following guidelines for choosing campsites will help you limit your impact.

Whenever possible, choose a heavily used site rather than create a new one. Further use of these camps will cause little additional damage. If there are no well-used sites, choose one that shows no sign of previous campers. Look for dense patches of dry grass, and avoid vegetated forest floors and areas with low-growing shrubs. If you are careful during your stay, the previously unused campsite will recover quickly and completely from your visit. Avoid the in-between sites—ones that have been used but still have substantial vegetation. These moderately impacted sites will recover if left alone, but will quickly deteriorate if used repeatedly.

In picking a campsite, consider whether it has a good solar aspect and whether it offers protection from wind and bugs. Envision how the site's sunshine or lack of it will affect your stay. Will you have morning sun? Evening sun? Shade at midday? A ray of sunlight hitting your tent makes it easier to get going on a frosty morning. Camping on the western side of a mountain or ridge can delay that ray for hours. In high, mountainous country and in the desert, the sun shines intensely during the summer. Does your camp have a place for you and your llamas to escape its blaze?

In the spring and summer, you will want to avoid mosquitos and flies by camping in as dry an area as possible. When the flies are bothersome, you might choose to camp on a knoll or hilltop where a breeze or wind will blow the flies away. Remember, you have a nylon screened tent; the llamas do not. Fighting flies burns lots of energy and can fatigue your llama more than packing a heavy load. In the fall, a camp protected from the wind will prove most hospitable.

Enjoy the view of the lake . . . but select a campsite at least 200 feet from water sources.

Llamas leave little impact on fragile wilderness areas.

Managing Your Herd in the Backcountry

Once you have chosen your campsite, tie the llamas near the site and remove the panniers and saddle. Canvas, nylon, and metal saddles can be placed over a log or in the branches of a tree for drying and storage. Leather saddles must be placed inside your tent at night to prevent squirrels and mice from chewing holes in them. Unpack the panniers and pile them under a tree or leave them out to be used as seat cushions at dinner. Leave the rest of the gear for now and take the llamas to a grazing site to be watered and fed.

Once you have found suitable grass at least 200 feet from camp, water and the trail, decide how best to keep your llamas so they will cause minimum damage but be catchable in the morning. There are three options—allowing them to roam free, building a corral, or picketing them.

The free-roaming llama will cause the least damage to the site. Before turning your stock loose, however, make sure you will be able to catch them in the morning. That means you need to know your llamas before turning them loose. If you are packing with an inse-

A leaning, dead tree makes a handy saddle rack in camp.

cure llama, he probably would not think of leaving camp. However, two llamas turned loose might take off down the trail together.

Personality, feed availability, experience, training, and personal attachment with the other llamas in camp are just a few of many factors that determine whether a llama will remain in camp. The best way to find out what your llama will do is to test him by turning him out. Leave the lead attached to his halter, and let the other end drag on the ground to hinder his forward movement as he avoids stepping on the line and to give you something to grab should he wander too far. Be sure there are no knots in the lead that could snag on a branch and break the llama's neck. Let him graze, but if he starts to mosey out of sight, approach him with grain and catch his lead.

If you have more than one llama, keep the most dominant one confined and turn the others loose (with their leads attached at first). After taking a few trips, your llamas will learn to stay around camp. Keep working at it. You, the llama, and the environment will all benefit from this approach.

The second-best method of stock management is the corral. Building permanent corrals is not a viable option in many backcountry areas. However, a temporary corral, such as a battery-operated electric fence, works well. Lightweight fiberglass poles and flexible

By staking one or two llamas, you can be sure the others will stick around camp.

This variation of the standard picket line works well in a meadow. Securely tie each llama to the long stakeout line far enough from neighboring llamas to prevent them from tangling their leads. By pulling up the pickets and moving the entire line, you can easily lead a group of llamas to new grazing.

Australian sheep fencing make a good, portable electric fence. (Introduce your llamas to electric fencing before you try it in the backcountry.) The temporary corral allows you to easily catch your stock in the morning but results in more trampling than if the llamas roamed freely.

The final option for confining llamas in camp is the picket stake. One simply screws the corkscrew-shaped picket stake into the earth and attaches a llama's lead to the stake. This method is the easiest, yet causes the most damage to the environment. One way to reduce the impact is to carry a lightweight, nylon webbing stake-out line, 25 to 30 feet long. Tied to the pickets, the long lines allow the llamas to roam over more ground, diluting their impact. With a little practice, the llamas will learn to negotiate the extra length of line.

Picket your stock clear of logs, stumps, trees, and other objects that might tangle the line. An open meadow is best. Also be sure to keep adjacent llamas far enough apart so they cannot tangle in another's lead line. An ac-quaintance of ours went packing with seven llamas and returned with only five because he didn't follow this rule. He staked his llamas too close together before leaving for a day hike, and when he returned, two llamas had strangled each other. Both of these llamas were experienced packers who had been staked out together many times before.

Whether corraled or picketed, the llamas frequently need to be moved to a new area. Do not let the animals mow the grass to the ground before moving them. Move them before the grass is eaten down to three inches in height.

Now that you have decided how to contain your llamas, feed and water them before returning to make camp. Llamas drink so little water that it is easiest—and causes less erosion along streams and lakes—to carry the gallon or so of water to the animals. Your llamas have probably burned lots of calories getting your gear to camp and should be fed. Use a high-sided container to reduce grain spillage. Grain is seed; spilling it allows non-native vegetation to spread in the backcountry.

Leave No Trace

With the llamas taken care of, you can get back to setting up camp. When camping in a heavily used site, set up in the center of the camp to avoid enlarging the abused area. In pristine campsites, spread out as much as possible to lessen the effects of trampling the vegetation and compacting the soil. Never use a pristine campsite more than one night. To minimize your impact on campsites, pay special attention to campfires, disposal of human and llama waste, and camping techniques in bear country.

After pitching the tent, avoid the urge to collect wood for an evening fire. Fire dam-ages the backcountry perhaps more than any other camping practice. Campfires have three negative effects on the backcountry. The fire sterilizes the soil beneath it, impeding recovery of vegetation. The campers trample vegetation and compact the soil around the campfire. Finally, gathering firewood alters the natural appearance of the campsite and surrounding area. Whenever possible, use a lightweight stove for meal preparation, and bring appropriate clothing to keep warm. Fires make more noise than you might realize, and a night spent sitting quietly in camp, watching the stars, is an experience you won't forget.

Permanent stock corrals have no place in the backcountry. Aside from marring the scenery, they concentrate stock use, resulting in soil compaction and trampled vegetation. It will take years for this campsite to recover from such abuse.

As destrucive as fires are, an occasional campfire is nice. If you decide to indulge in the luxury of a campfire, do it safely, causing as little damage as possible. If you camp in a high-use area, use an existing fire ring. In a pristine area, select a site that is rocky or sandy, has exposed mineral soil, or is below high waterline of a stream or river. Before going to bed or breaking camp, make sure the fire is out, then thinly scatter the ashes a short distance from camp, making them as inconspicuous as possible.

Another technique we use is to carefully cut a circle of sod out of the ground. Dig the circle deep enough to include the topsoil, likely six or ten inches deep in the forest. Cut around the edge of the circle with a shovel, then lift the intact circle out. Build your fire in this pit. When you leave the campsite, you can spread the dead ashes and replace the circle. The sod you replace will contain viable seeds that have not been affected by the fire's heat. If you are careful, you can almost completely hide the traces of your fire from the next campers.

A cook stove can be worth its weight in gold. Whether you use propane or white gas for fuel, you can adjust the flame to suit your

Destruction at a fire ring. Trampled ground and sawed logs remain long after the campers have left the site. (Note: not an Ecollama campsite.)

cooking needs—and the stove is easy to light even in the rain (something you can't say for the campfire.)

The disadvantages of packing a cookstove are obvious—extra weight and having to deal with the fuel. New stoves on the market have helped with the weight problem. The two burner, compact propane stove we use weighs only 10 pounds. We prefer propane because it has none of the fuel spills and associated fumes of white gas. Small (2 ¼ pounds when full), refillable propane tanks will last three days—cooking six meals for four people. We usually take a couple of these and use the campfire for boiling water for noodles and dishwater.

We can further reduce our impact around camp by properly managing our waste, both human and llama. Take care of human waste by urinating on rocks or in non-vegetated areas far from water sources and by using latrines or outhouses if they exist. Lacking a latrine or outhouse, dig and use a small cat-hole less than six inches deep. If you dig too deep the feces will not break down quickly. Burn the toilet paper either in the hole or in a campfire ring so rodents or bears will not dig it up.

The portable kitchen with gas stove leaves little or no trace in a backcountry campsite.

When we are camping with a group of people, we use a neat little trick that keeps the campers happy. We tie a handkerchief on a branch above the latrine and keep the shovel in camp. If the handkerchief or the shovel is missing, the latrine is occupied. We also hang a plastic bag at the latrine to collect the paper waste to pack out, a good practice, especially when camping with a group.

Llama feces, although visually much like deer or elk feces, also require attention. Keep them out of camp, and spread accumulated llama feces with a kick of your boot. This will discourage flies and prevent any concentrated odor.

By taking special care you can prevent water pollution in the wilderness. Keep human and llama waste well away from streams and lakes. Always use biodegradable soap for washing dishes and bathing. To bathe yourself, gather some water in a bucket or pot and walk away from the source before lathering and rinsing. Scatter water from bathing and dirty dishes as widely as possible, away from camp and water sources.

Campers must take special precautions when camping in bear country. Whether there are black bears or grizzly bears, you must secure your food so the bears cannot raid it. Besides ruining your trip, having your food eaten by a bear is also bad for the bruin. After tasting human food, a bear is more apt to approach or even attack humans and becomes a "problem bear" that may eventually have to be killed.

Set up your cooking area 100 feet, preferably downwind, from your tents. You do not want the scent of the food wafting past your tent. At night and while you are away from camp during the day, suspend your food between two trees that are at least twenty feet apart. Try to get the food fifteen feet off the ground to keep it out of bears' reach. Plastic buckets with a wire bail handle, such as the ones restaurants order bulk tomato sauce or pickles in, work well for hanging food. Hang food in an area at least 100 feet from your sleeping and cooking areas.

Try to confine your llamas in an open area when camping in bear country. This will reduce the probability of a surprise attack and will give the llamas and the bear a chance to size each other up. Be sure to have a shock absorber (such as rubber tubing) somewhere in the stakeout line. That way if a bear charges, the llamas can get away without breaking their necks. For references with more detailed information about camping and precautions for camping in bear country, see the Appendix.

After you pack up and prepare to move on, take one more look around. Is the fire completely out? Is all the trash picked up? Did you remember to collect all the llamas' picket stakes and feed buckets? If you are a conscientious llama packer, the place will look as if no one had ever been there.

– 10 –

LLAMA FIRST AID

We begin this chapter with a caveat: The following pages will not make you a llama veterinarian. You will, however, learn to treat the more common problems that might develop on a llama pack trip. Of course, your best protection is preventing accident and injury and detecting problems early, before they become serious.

We once noticed a llama who was not eating on the trail. We imagined all sorts of horrendous possible causes for his behavior, from plant poisoning to a broken jaw or abscessed tooth. We quickly found the source of the problem. It was only our first day out, but an overly snug halter had worn sore spots on both sides of the llama's lower jaw. The simple solution required that we switch halters and apply some cream to the sore spots. However, it could have easily developed into abcesses and infection if we had not noticed the problem right away.

There are inherent risks to being out on the trail that you must accept if you wish to experience the joys of packing with your llama. Packing a year's worth of veterinary supplies will not eliminate the risks. Accepting the risks while using common sense, carefully observing your llamas, and packing a small but versatile first aid kit will go a long way toward reducing them.

Two types of situations require backcountry first aid: injuries (including sore foot pads) and gastrointestinal upsets. Add to this dehydration or heat exhaustion, due to poor conditioning, and tick and snake bites, and you will have covered just about any backcountry circumstance that will require first aid. In any of these situations, catching the problem early will go a long way towards curing it. Not catching the problem early may result in infection or pneumonia. Knowledge of human first aid will help you provide appropriate treatment for your llama on the trail.

Symptoms of an ill llama include poor appetite, constant humming, dull eyes, drooping head, or rounded back.

Know Your First Aid Kit

Our veterinarian has a first aid kit that he lends for backcountry use. It is well-stocked with items that can treat both human and livestock ailments. He offers it for free; the borrowers pay only for the items they use. More often than not, the kit is used for human first aid needs, such as minor scrapes and burns. Check with your vet to see if a "loaner" first aid kit is an option for you. Assembling your own complete kit can cost over $300, making the loaner kit a very attractive alternative.

Whichever route you choose, become thoroughly familiar with the contents of the kit and how to administer all medications. These are some helpful tips:

- Review the contents of the kit with your vet so you will know how to use each item properly before you have an emergency on the trail.

- Consult with your veterinarian for proper doses of the medications in your first aid kit. Keep a list of dosages in the kit.

- Know the approximate weights of your animals so that you can administer proper doses.

The most complete first-aid kit in the world may prove useless if you do not know how to administer its contents. You can even make the situation worse through improper first aid. So use caution, common sense, and knowledge in giving first aid. Provide only a minimum amount of treatment, just enough to get you and your llama home safely.

Making Your Own First Aid Kit

The following list describes a basic first aid kit useful in most situations. It includes several multi-purpose items. Check with other local llama packers and your veterinarian for additional suggestions. Then modify the kit to meet your own needs.

1. Antibacterial cream (such as nitrofurasone cream or betadine ointment). Apply it to wounds in a thin layer.

2. 4"x4" gauze pads

3. Elasticon bandage (Ace bandage) and Vet Wrap (self-adhesive). Pull the Ace bandage to one-third its stretch when wrapping unless there is padding beneath it.

4. Duct tape. An all-purpose, handy item to have along.

5. Sheet cotton and diaper pins. Sheet cotton (diapers, pillow case, etc.) provides support, prevents pressure sores, and prevents further swelling if applied correctly.

6. Ophthalmic ointment (without a steroid), such as Neosporin ointment. Apply three to six times daily, depending upon the severity of the injury, for bruises or chafed areas.

First aid kit from the veterinarian includes stapler (for quick repair of skin tears) and medications available only through a veterinarian.

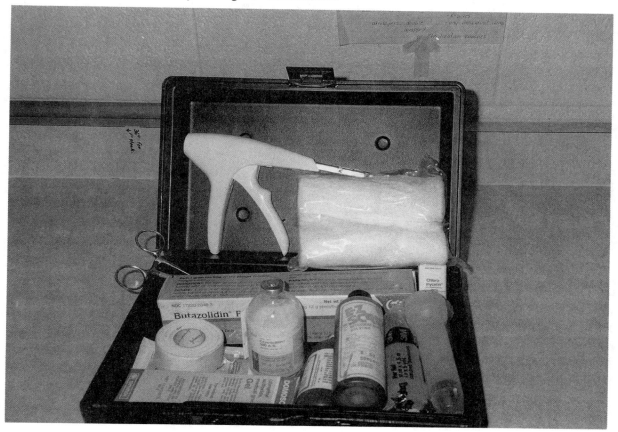

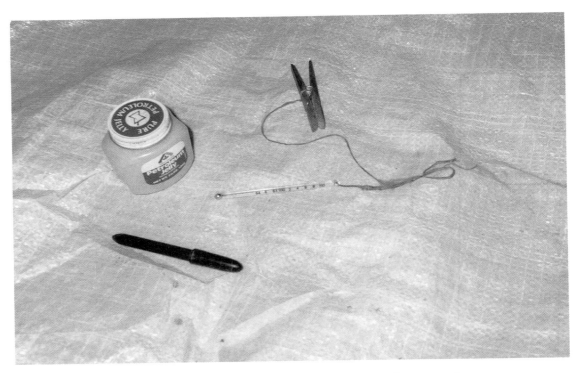

Thermometer with string and clothespin to clip to wool.

7. Surgical scrub, such as Nolvasan or Betadine skin cleanser. Use a surgical scrub soap after you remove any obvious debris in the wound. Use scrub sparingly to cleanse the wound prior to bandaging. Rinse the wound thoroughly after cleansing.

8. Rubbing alcohol (isopropyl alcohol, 95%) for disinfecting and cooling.

9. Flashlight

10. Thermometer (rectal). A llama's normal temperature is between 99 and 102 degrees Fahrenheit depending on the animal's age and level of activity. Hypothermia (sub-normal temperatures) and hyperthermia (elevated temperatures) can result from plant poisoning or exhaustion. Tie a string with a clothespin to the end of the thermometer; clip the pin to the wool while taking your llama's temperature.

11. Anti-inflammatory pain killer, such as flunixin (Banamine oral paste or injectable) or phenylbutazone paste (antiprostaglandin). We suggest Banamine oral paste. Follow veterinarian's dosage instructions. Injectable banamine is also available.

12. Mineral oil or regular vegetable cooking oil to be used only in severe poisoning cases. There is a risk in administering the oil—it can go down the wrong tube into their lungs instead of their stomach. Review the procedure with your vet. Give one quart orally for an adult llama. A trained person can use a stomach tube or you can give about one cup at a time using

a plastic beverage bottle. Hold the llama's head and tip the nose up as you pour the oil in the side of the llama's mouth. You can also try mixing the oil with grain.

13. Milk of Magnesia (or powdered oral antacid, such as Maalox). Give two to three ounces orally every three hours for plant poisoning. Three doses should be enough; frequent use is the key to this product. You should see improvement twenty minutes after the first dose.

14. Stomach tube and speculum for tubing (see #13 above)

15. Ivermectin (injectable or pour on). Administer in the event of tick paralysis. This is a worming medicine that will cause any remaining ticks to stop sucking and fall off. The injectable form will work faster in an emergency. Under the skin, inject 1 cc. per 110 pounds of body weight.

16. Syringes, sterile needles.

17. Foot bootie (for sore pads or injury to pads)

18. Scissors

19. Paper towels

20. Nose tube to keep nasal passages open in event of snake bite on the face.

21. Tribrissen oral antibiotic (oral paste). Follow veterinarian's suggested dosage. May need to be given twice a day for at least six days.

Dehydration and Hyperthermia
(Exhaustion and Heat Stress)

Llamas have more difficulty keeping cool than staying warm and commonly suffer from dehydration and hyperthermia, or heat stress. The usual symptoms include heavy breathing, foaming at the mouth, a lack of muscle coordination, and overall weakness.

To treat dehydration or hyperthermia, remove the llama's pack and let him rest. Check his temperature. (Normal temperature is between 99 and 102 degrees Fahrenheit.) Give him plenty of water, and if possible, attempt to cool him by walking him in a stream or wetting his skin. Simply throwing a bucket of water over him will not help, as his wool will shed the water. Cool him by spraying areas of exposed skin such as his belly and between his legs. In extreme cases, you can give a cold water enema, but then you lose the ability to monitor his rectal temperature. Applying alcohol to his exposed skin (belly, inner sides of legs) will also cool him. Try to keep him standing to allow more air circulation.

To prevent heat stress, properly condition your llama before packing, provide frequent access to water and shade in hot weather, and observe him carefully while hiking. Watch for rapid, shallow breathing. If you are hiking behind a llama, your first clue of hyperthermia may be an unsteadiness in his rear legs. The llama's belly will be moving rapidly with each breath, and he will seem unable to catch his breath. If you can let your llama rest completely, stand in water, and lighten his load, you can avoid the onset of full-blown heat stress.

In a severe case—your llama has collapsed and can only stand for a short time—administer orally or inject Banamine or other pain killer to help reduce muscle fatigue so that the llama can move a short distance to water or camp.

After the intial treatment, an overnight rest with normal feed and water will usually bring full recovery. Lay over another day if necessary, and load the animal lightly, if at all, until you are sure he has recovered fully.

A thoroughly exhausted llama may suffer from myositis-exhaustion complex, which can be difficult to distinguish from gastrointestinal upset. In fact, they may occur together. The complex may be brought on by abnormally hot weather, a young, overweight, or overfed llama that is overburdened for his condition, or a heavily muscled young llama that is overburdened, though large, for his age. Myositis-exhaustion complex causes muscle cramping and inflammation. A llama in this condition will be weak, quiver, drag his feet, and show other signs of muscle fatigue.

Take the llama's temperature, and treat as you would for heat stress (above). To cool his body temperature, you can also administer Banamine (oral paste painkiller) and Milk of Magnesia. Let your llama rest, and offer him water. You will likely have to remove all of his load. This llama needs medical attention as soon as possible. If you are out in the woods and the llama has not been severely affected, he may be capable of walking out without a load after several days of rest.

Indigestion

Gastrointestinal upsets (colic) usually result from a change in routine that produces stress. Changes in feed or exercise, a new environment, new animals, being transported, or parasites are likely causes. An animal suffering from colic may show signs of abdominal pain, abdominal distension, no appetite, constipation, diarrhea, and convulsions. Treat with Banamine, Milk of Magnesia, rest, and water.

Plant poisoning may also cause gastrointestinal upsets. You can usually identify the poisonous plant if you examine the area where your llama was tethered. Signs of poisoning appear in two to twenty-four hours, depending on the amount eaten. Most llamas show the same signs as those listed above for colic, with the possible addition of uncoordination and salivation. We recently had an animal on a spring training hike who returned home drooling and even vomited cud. We gave him a series of doses of Maalox antacid, and he perked right up within twenty minutes of the first dose. This was not a severe case of plant poisoning, and the animal recovered immediately.

Other treatments include Banamine, activated charcoal (not included in our basic first aid kit because it is difficult to administer), mineral oil (one quart), and Milk of Magnesia (two to three ounces given orally every three hours). The charcoal and mineral oil are used only in very severe cases. One dose of the charcoal is probably sufficient, but give Milk of Magnesia frequently and Banamine every eight hours.

A llama who has eaten poisonous plants may need as much as a week to fully recover, but will probably be able to walk back to the trailhead within a day or two. Ask Forest Service authorities or check with your local county U. S. D. A. Extension office for a list of poisonous plants in your area and their identifying features. Familiarize yourself with these plants so you can avoid unknowingly tethering your llama near them. The Appendix lists references for poisonous plants.

Your llama will not need a book to identify poisonous plants along the trail and will usually avoid eating them.

Wounds and Injuries

Treat a llama's wounds as you would treat human injuries. The following guidelines will help:

1. Remain calm; panicking will only worsen the situation.

2. If the llama begins hemorrhaging, try to stop the bleeding with pressure.

3. Clean the wound with a surgical scrub and water. Do not waterlog it. Dry with towels.

4. Clip the hair around the wound so you can see what you are doing.

5. Consider the anatomy of the injured area for possible damage to joints, bones, tendons, or internal organs.

Among the injuries your llama may suffer out on the trail are saddle and cinch sores, bruised or cut foot pads, lacerations, rope burns, sprains, and fractures.

Saddle and cinch sores are easy to prevent and slow to heal. Take extra care putting on the saddle, breast straps, cruppers, and halter to avoid creating a problem. Always check the wool in the saddle area for burrs or other irritants. A llama who balks on the trail may be trying to alert you to problems with his rigging.

Bruised or cut foot pads may require an improvised bootie to protect the foot and allow the llama to walk.

Most simple injuries can be splinted or treated just as you would comparable human injuries. For the more serious injuries, such as broken limbs, you must consider seeking help. Some people have even had their llamas helicoptered out of the backcountry. If your llama has broken any limbs, do not move him. At some point, you may realize your llama cannot be helped and must make the hard decision to put an end to his suffering.

Snake Bites and Ticks

In some parts of North America snakes and ticks are severe problems. The llama packer should ask if poisonous snakes are in the area before heading into the backcountry. Although snakes are shy creatures generally, llamas are so curious that they will put their noses down to investigate the snake and get bitten in the face. Ticks, on the other hand, are not shy at all and come aboard uninvited. However, ticks are usually a seasonal problem that cause little harm if removed early. Nevertheless, bites from both snakes and ticks can be fatal to llamas and you should be prepared to treat them.

Snake bites usually occur around the face and legs, normally presenting no threat to the your llama's life. However, if the llama is bitten in the nose, swelling may obstruct the nasal passages. Since llamas generally breath through their noses, not their mouths, a snake bite on the nose may impede breathing. Cold cloths placed over or around the affected area may help reduce swelling from a bite on the face. Placing a tube in the nostril will allow the llama to breath normally. An empty barrel of a ball-point pen can substitute for a tube if needed. (Nose tube is included as item #20 in First Aid Kit above.)

For bites on the legs, concentrate on minimizing and reducing swelling by walking the llama in a stream. Consult with your veterinarian for proper treatment, depending upon what venomous snakes are in your area.

Ticks can carry many potentially serious diseases, but tick paralysis, which is potentially fatal, is the most common. Approximately 40 percent of all female ticks release a toxin in their saliva that causes paralysis in the animal they bite. Ticks can cause severe illness or death if the symptoms are not recognized promptly, but if removed early, ticks create only mild problems.

The severity of the reaction will depend upon the type, location, and number of ticks infesting your llama. The symptoms of tick paralysis include gradual loss of muscle control. At first, the animal may just be cranky and lie down frequently. Then he will want to lie down almost constantly, appearing unsteady when he gets up. Eventually his entire body, including his lungs, will be paralyzed, leading to death.

Removing the tick (or ticks) is the only way to help the llama. Favorite banquet areas for ticks include the chest, armpits (front and rear), the upper thighs, the head, upper neck, behind the ears, under the tail, and around the sheath. Remove the tick with a slow, steady pull that will not break off its mouthparts. Crush the tick with a rock or stick (not your fingers) after removal. Immediately treat the bite area on the llama with antiseptic, such as alcohol or betadine. A mildly affected llama will show signs of recovery within six hours after the tick is removed. After handling a tick, wash your hands well to prevent the spread of any infectious diseases the tick might have been carrying.

If your llama becomes seriously ill, you may need to shear him to the skin to make sure you have found all the ticks. Even if you are certain you have found all the ticks, it is wise to give a shot of Ivermectin wormer (1 cc.

per 110 pounds, under the skin). The Ivermectin will take up to twelve hours to affect any remaining ticks.

You can lessen the risk of tick paralysis by treating your llamas with a topical insecticide. We have found application of the sheep product Ectrin helps discourage ticks. Mix the Ectrin with water to a 0.25% solution, and pour about a cup down the back of each llama's neck and spine once a week or just before departing on a pack trip. Be cautious of any systemic insecticide, as it likely has not been tested on llamas. Avoid using any insecticide on pregnant female llamas.

Although accidents can happen, common sense and good preparation will keep them to a minimum.

Recognizing the possible dangers your llama faces in the backcountry is the first step in keeping your llama healthy and happy. Llamas usually keep out of trouble on their own, but observing your animal carefully will alert you to a problem before it becomes serious.

We have been fortunate to have experienced only a few minor scrapes in the backcountry and, with the exception of tick paralysis and mild plant poisoning, have not had to deal with the more serious situations described above. We have gleaned the suggested treatments from a variety of sources—mostly from other llama packers, Dr. Rollett Pruyn (our llama veterinarian), and a talk given by Dr. LaRue Johnson on Backcountry First Aid at the 1989 International Llama Association Conference. Dr. Johnson's favorite remedies include "a tincture of time and an ounce of prevention." We would add a goodly supply of duct tape.

Sometimes the llama has an easier time crossing streams than the hiker.

– 11 –

FOOD FOR THOUGHT
Backcountry Cooking

Of all the conveniences packing with llamas offers, none gives more pleasure than the ability to carry fresh foods. Gone are the days of granola for breakfast, gorp for lunch, and some freeze-dried concoction for dinner. With llamas carrying the food, we can indulge ourselves with fresh fruits, vegetables, and delicious dinners. However, a word of caution: food is important, but if you end up spending most of your time around camp preparing and cooking food, you might as well stay home.

To best use our four-legged caterers, we need to learn which foods travel well, how to pack the food so it lasts, how to prepare the meals, and how to store food while in camp.

Menu Please: What to Take

The options are endless. We recommend meals that are fairly lightweight and nutritional, yet fully satisfying and filling. The following questions and suggestions will help you plan tasty, healthful meals.

1. Will you want to eat this food after hiking all day? If it doesn't sound appetizing, don't bring it.

2. How much food preparation will each meal or food require? Can you imagine yourself cooking it after hiking all day? If it sounds like a lot of work, opt for a different meal or choice of food.

3. Be resourceful and creative. For example, alternate rice, noodles, dried mashed potatoes, spaghetti, bread, and corn tortillas for variety in the carbohydrate-rich, filling foods you eat on the trail.

4. Plan balanced meals—remember to include fruits and vegetables.

5. Eat perishables early in the trip and long-lasting foods later in the trip.

6. Prepare all your recipes at home before including them in a backcountry menu. Or better yet, adapt your favorite recipes to backcountry cooking. Pre-measure and pre-mix ingredients at home whenever possible to simplify cooking in camp.

7. Check out the backpacking ingredients at your local health food store, and try them before taking them on the trail. Our meals regularly include dried tofu, dried tomato paste, instant dried refried beans, cheddar cheese powder, dried lemon powder (no sugar), dried onions, powdered milk, and dried fruits. We also buy soup mixes, spices, and herbs in bulk at our local store to refill the containers that fit into our special kitchen boxes. This reduces the amount of store packaging we throw away.

If you can't find these foods in your area, The Good Food Store in Missoula, Montana, offers many dried foods on a mail order basis. For a complete list write: 920 Kensington, Missoula, MT 59801, or call (406) 728-5823.

Packing and Preparing the Food

As important as selecting the right foods for your trip is preparing and packing the food so it is still edible when you reach camp. You can't easily harm a can of sardines, but a dozen eggs or a bag of chips require more care. We carry our food in square plastic buckets, putting two in each pannier. When loading the food into the panniers or coolers, we use the same method the checkout clerks at the local grocery store use. Heavy, hard items (sardines and cans of tuna fish) go on the bottom with softer lighter items (bread, chips, cookies) on top.

We pack one bucket as a freezer and another as a refrigerated container and insulate both by wrapping each bucket in insulating foam, such as a foam sleeping pad. There is no need to carry ice or frozen ice packs. Simply prepare a dish and freeze it to serve as the ice. On the day you plan to serve a pre-frozen meal, transfer it from the freezer to the refrigerated container so it will defrost by dinnertime. When packing your coolers, remember that cold air sinks. Placing the coldest items on top will cool the entire container as the cold air circulates to the bottom of the container.

To save packing space, use as many non-rigid containers for carrying the food as possible. Pack coffee and tang, for example, in plastic zip-closure bags to eliminate the weight and bulk of glass containers. Toss out the instant oatmeal and hot cocoa boxes, and pack the individual packets wherever they fit. Medium-sized eggs travel and keep well (if left in their shells) in the plastic egg carriers sold in camping stores. If you're going to scramble the eggs anyway, do it at home, then store the mixture in a tightly sealed plastic container in your refrigerated bucket until mealtime.

Figuring out how much food to take is difficult. Some cookbooks suggest allowing 1/4 pound of meat per person for a meal. But if someone is hungry they will eat two or even three servings. The only thing worse than having to pack out half of your load of food is to run short. We carry between two and two and a half pounds of food per person per day on our commercial pack trips.

Cooking in the backcountry can be as easy as cooking at home if you have planned well and prepared as much food as possible before leaving home. The need for organization is exacerbated by the lack of counter space. Prepare all food before you start cooking. Otherwise the eggs of your omelet will be done before you

We can count on finding patches of snow for storing perishable food items in the high country of Montana during the summer.

have a chance to add the cheese and onions. Plan ahead where you will put cooked food, and serve it up as soon as you are done cooking so it stays hot.

If you are cooking at elevations above 7,000 feet you will need to allow extra cooking time.

At sea level water boils at 212 degrees F. At higher elevations it boils at a lower temperature. Cooking noodles in the mountains takes longer because the boiling water supplies less heat.

Storing Food

Proper backcountry food storage keeps the wildlife out of your chow and reduces spoilage. Small rodents can quickly consume or destroy your food, ruining or cutting short your stay. Large animals like bears and coyotes may become dangerous once they taste human food. Just because you can't see the animals doesn't mean they aren't there. If you always act as though they are there, you and your food should be safe.

Store your food in secure wooden or metal boxes or lidded plastic buckets to discourage furry raiders. Don't make the mistake of storing food in your panniers or tent. Rodents will chew through leather, canvas, and cordura nylon to reach a tasty treat.

When camping in bear country, take special precautions to protect yourself and your food. Before going to bed or leaving camp for a day hike, hang the food in a tree. Grizzly bears are not good tree climbers, but they do have a good reach. In grizzly country, hang the food at least fifteen feet high in a single tree. Black bears are adept tree climbers, so in black bear country, suspend the food on a rope between two trees. The supporting trees need to be twenty feet apart, and the load fifteen feet off the ground. Check with the land manager where you will be camping for specific bear behavior in that area.

To keep your food from spoiling find a cool place for it between meals. The areas we visit have snow patches all summer long. We store our food in plastic buckets with handles so we can easily carry the food from the eating area to the snowbank refrigerator. We simply dig a hole in the snow and insert the bucket. Place snow on top of the bucket and shade it to keep the food cooler.

If no snow is available, place the container in a creek to keep it cool. Make sure the container will not fall over and that no water can enter. We place a heavy stone on top of the container to keep it from floating away. Desert pack trips with no cool storage will require an appropriate menu.

Remember most meals taste good in the woods. Eat well and go light!

Plastic food buckets with wire handles work well for food storage, and also double as seats.

What's For Dinner?

What are some of your favorite, quick and easy meals to prepare at home? You can probably adapt these meals for use in your trail menu. If you are planning a long excursion you will need to give much more thought and consideration to weight and menu than on a typical four- or five-day trip. A typical four-day menu in the backcountry might include hot and cold cereals for two breakfasts, pancakes, and French toast. Lunches might start out with sandwich meat and cheeses, then go to canned salmon, salami, cheese and crackers, and peanut butter and jelly later in the week. Cookies and fresh fruit round out the lunches. See the Appendix for a sample five-day menu.

After you have planned your menu, think through the process of cooking each recipe and eating each meal. Write a complete shopping list and "to bring" list as you think through the meals. This way, you will be sure to bring everything necessary, including salt and pepper, cooking oil to stir-fry vegetables, coffee,

Trout for dinner.

enough pots and pans to make each dish, and other essentials. Items such as seasonings and cooking oil are very easy to forget because you take them for granted when they are in the cupboard at home. It is tough to stretch the butter or margarine meant for toast and sandwiches into enough cooking fat for a five-day trip.

Keep It Simple

We focus on serving good, home-cooked evening meals, but that doesn't mean we do all the cooking on the trail. For example, on the first night in camp, after hiking all day, we want a quick and easy dinner. To prepare for this, we cook a mixture of ground turkey and ground beef with Mexican seasonings at home and freeze it. On the trail, the meat serves as ice in our coolers. When we get to camp we heat it up, break out the chips and salsa, lettuce, cheese, tomatoes, tortillas, refried beans, and sour cream, and dinner is ready. Plan on big appetites this first night in camp. If you have leftover tortillas and beans, they will likely disappear at breakfast the next morning.

As commercial outfitters, we try to provide choices such as vegetarian options and lighter seasoning. In the Mexican meal outlined above, someone could easily skip the meat and still have a well-balanced meal with beans and cheese. We season mildly and provide salsa so that people can add extra spice if they choose.

We also plan some flexibility in the menus to allow for fresh trout and other delicacies—but be sure to have a backup plan if the fish aren't biting. For example, you can make a basic sherry/cream sauce and put it over noodles with canned salmon or omit the salmon and substitute fresh trout with the noodles. If you have leftover sour cream from the night before, you can add that to the noodles as well.

Some Other Favorites

When cooking for a group, consider using a wok for stir-frying. Stir-fried vegetables with spicy Szechuan chicken is one of our favorites and we have included the recipe at the end of this chapter. Zucchini, green onions, and mushrooms travel very well for stir-fry, and you can add any tomatoes that have had a rough trip. If you cook the vegetables and chicken separately and serve with rice, you preserve the option of a vegetarian menu. Lettuce and a slice of homebaked bread complete the meal.

Pasta with a variety of sauces makes a great-tasting camp meals. We prepare pesto with basil from our garden to serve with spaghetti. We also cook meatballs at home and freeze them in an herb and tomato sauce. On the trail, we heat the meatballs and mix dry tomato paste to increase the amount of sauce. We offer the two sauces with the spaghetti for meat and meatless options.

Curry dishes, Brazilian black bean soup, and Chinese hot and sour soup are also favorites for the trail. We have included the soup recipes so you can try them out for yourself.

For desserts, we bake zucchini, pumpkin, banana, or applesauce breads for our trips. These moist breads freeze well and then stay fresh until the last day of a five-day trip. We give everyone a snack pack with fruit leather, gorp, and candy bars to carry with them and eat when they want to. Puddings (from a mix), brownies, lots of cookies, dried fruits, and even cheese cake (from a mix) are all welcome after-dinner treats. Once we baked and packed a pecan pie for a special guest on a trip—it traveled amazingly well.

saddle. One llama carries the entire kitchen—both wooden boxes.

If you are at all handy with tools, you can easily build a set of kitchen pannier boxes this winter. Aluminum, lightweight and sturdy, is probably the best material, but it is very expensive and requires special tools and skills. Wood is less expensive and more forgiving of mistakes during construction. One-eighth-inch-thick plywood makes a lightweight and strong box.

After measuring several standard llama panniers on the market, we chose outside dimensions for our boxes of 16 inches high, 22 inches long, and 12 inches deep. This size will work for most llamas. Ripping a three-quarter-inch-thick board into three-quarter inch strips will supply you with framing material. The three-quarter-inch square framing provides strength without taking up too much inside space. Use glue and screws to attach the plywood to the frame.

Our panniers' opening doors allow one to serve as a cupboard and the other as a storage compartment. You may choose a different arrangement to better accommodate your kitchen ware.

Once you have built the boxes, you will need to devise a way to connect them to the llama. The simplest way is to drill two holes in each box on the side that will ride next to the llama. Drill the holes about five inches below the top of the box, allowing the same amount of space between the holes as is between the front and rear crossarms on the sawbuck saddle. Then bolt two one-inch-wide nylon straps with a heavy-duty grommet in one end to the box. The other end of the strap can be made into a loop, using a fastex buckle.

Kitchen boxes travel well on a sawbuck saddle. The grill rides on top on one side, the aluminum camp stand on the other side.

Other Kitchen Paraphernalia

The kitchen pannier boxes are important—but useless without quality contents. What you pack for kitchenware depends on the type of meals you are serving. We have supplied a list of the wares we use as a reference—add and delete appropriately.

We strongly recommend stocking your kitchen with reusable cups, plates, and flatware. Paper plates don't need to be washed, but even the best paper plates get soggy and fold mid-meal. Paper and foam cups are thin, making hot drinks hard to hold without burning yourself. Even worse is what these products do to the environment. Although trees are a renewable resource, the very forest you are visiting may need to be clear-cut someday to provide more paper plates and cups. Further, the manufacturing of foam releases chloroflourocarbons (CFCs) into the atmosphere. Scientists have shown that CFCs deplete the ozone, the layer in our atmosphere that protects us from the sun's harmful ultraviolet rays. Isn't it worth washing a few dishes?

We have had great luck with Corelle brand plates. They don't scratch like plastic plates and are nearly indestructible. The best, affordable cup we have found is a thick plastic mug sold at K-MART. Metal cups conduct too much heat, cooling their contents quickly and burning lips. Insulated stainless mugs are nice but cost over ten dollars apiece.

One kitchen accessory we have found invaluable is our Coleman collapsible stand. It weighs only a pound and folds into a very compact unit. The aluminum stand holds our cupboard out of the dust without requiring construction of a temporary log or rock shelf.

Peanut butter and jelly served with a side of beans may be standard fare for the backpacker. But with a llama carrying our backcountry kitchen, we have the culinary freedom to enjoy a wide variety of flavorful dishes. I hope you take advantage of the opportunity to indulge in the backcountry. Just remember—you can get good food at almost any restaurant, but there's only one place that serves wilderness.

From the Kitchen of Ecollama

Hot and Sour Soup (4 servings)

1 package Lipton Chicken noodle soup (or other noodle soup mix)
½ cup sliced pitted California ripe olives
½ cup sliced green onions
½ cup diced tofu (Mori-Nu brand tofu does not need refrigeration)
1 tablespoon cornstarch
1 beaten egg
1 tablespoon rice vinegar or white vinegar
1 teaspoon sesame oil
⅛ teaspoon cayenne pepper

Heat soup mix with 1 quart of boiling water. Add olives, green onions, and tofu. Blend cornstarch with ¾ cup water and then add to soup. Heat soup to boiling, stirring constantly until mixture thickens slightly.

Remove from heat. Slowly pour beaten egg into soup while stirring gently in one direction. Stir in remaining ingredients before serving (these can be pre-mixed at home in a small container).

Serve with tabasco sauce for seasoning individual servings.

Brazilian Black Bean Soup (4 one-cup servings)

2 tablespoons butter or oil
1 medium onion, chopped
1 or 2 cloves garlic, minced
butter or oil
1-7 ounce package instant black beans (Fantastic Foods brand)
salsa
green pepper (optional)

In a large soup pot, saute onion, garlic, and green pepper in butter or oil until softened.

Add 4 cups water plus instant black beans and bring to a boil. Add salsa to taste.

Lower heat to medium. Cover and cook for 5 to 10 minutes. Serve topped with sour cream.

Szechuan Chicken and Stir-Fry Vegetables (4 servings)

1 egg white, lightly beaten
1 tablespoon cornstarch
2 chicken breasts, boned, skinned and cut into ½ inch strips
oil
1 tablespoon red peppers (dried)
1 cup unsalted dry roasted peanuts
¼ cup sliced green onions
¼ cup soy sauce
¼ cup light corn syrup or honey
2 tablespoons dry white wine

Mix egg white with cornstarch. Use this mixture to lightly coat chicken strips.

Heat oil in frying pan and add red peppers. Stir fry 10 seconds. Add chicken mixture and stir fry 3 to 5 minutes until chicken turns white. Stir in peanuts, green onions, soy sauce, corn syrup or honey, and wine (these last three ingredients can be pre-mixed at home).

Stirring constantly bring to a boil and boil 1 minute.

Garnish with green onions and serve with rice and stir-fried vegetables (zucchini, tomatoes, onions, green peppers, mushrooms).

Tabouli Salad (6 half-cup servings)

1 cup bulgur wheat
1½ teaspoons salt
¼ cup lemon juice
1 teaspoon crushed garlic
½ teaspoon dry mint
¼ cup good olive oil
pepper
½ cup chopped green onions
2 medium tomatoes, diced
1 cup (packed) chopped parsley
feta cheese (optional)
cucumbers (optional)
black olives (optional)

Add the bulghur wheat to 1½ cups boiling water and salt. Cover, remove from heat and let sit 20 minutes.

Add the lemon, garlic, mint, oil, and pepper. Refrigerate several hours or overnight.

Just before serving (on the trail), add green onions, diced tomatoes, and parsley. Add feta cheese, cucumber, and olives if desired.

Ecologic Rye Bread (2 oblong loaves)

This family recipe was developed through trial and error and has become a regular treat on Ecollama trips. We bake it at home the night before a trek and eat it the first day on the trail while it is still fresh.

2 cups warm water
1½ tablespoons yeast
1 tablespoon sugar
1 tablespoon salt
½ cup rye flour
3 tablespoons caraway seeds
5 to 6 cups bread flour (can substitute 1 to 2 cups whole wheat bread flour for 1 to 2 cups of white flour)
3 tablespoons cornmeal
1 tablespoon egg white

Mix together water, yeast, and sugar. When the mixture is bubbly, add salt, rye flour, and caraway seeds. (Optional ingredients that can be added at this point: ¼ cup wheat germ; ¼ cup rolled rye flakes, wheat bran, or oat bran; ¼ cup steel-cut oats; or additional rye flour to your taste. Variations also include sourdough starter, ½ cup plain yogurt, and ¼ cup oil if you want to keep it fresh longer.)

Add the rest of the flour and knead for 8 to 10 minutes. Place the dough in a greased bowl, cover, and let rise 1 hour. (Note: Expect this bread to be somewhat sticky due to the rye flour, add only enough flour to make it easy to handle.)

After doubled, punch down and let rise again (less time than first rising). Punch down and shape into 2 oblong rye loaves.

Sprinkle cornmeal on an ungreased baking sheet. Place loaves on sheet and cover. Let rise 20 minutes. Slash tops and brush with egg white mixed with 1 tablespoon cold water.

Put in cold oven and bake 35 minutes at 400 degrees until brown. Serve warm with unsalted butter.

Banana Bread (1 loaf)

2 eggs
1 cup sugar
3 ripe bananas*
2 cups flour
1 teaspoon soda
Pinch of salt
½ cup melted shortening

Preheat oven to 300 degrees F.

Mix ingredients in bowl. Bake approximately 1 hour in greased loaf pan. Let cool before removing from pan. Freezes and travels well.

*Note: Can substitute 1 cup of applesauce for bananas.

Zucchini Bread (2 to 3 medium loaves, 1 large and 1 small loaf, or 36 muffins)

2 cups zucchini (grated)
3 eggs
1 cup sugar
1 cup oil
½ teaspoon salt
2 teaspoon cinnamon
1 teaspoon baking soda
½ teaspoon baking powder
3 cups flour
½ cup nuts
3 teaspoon vanilla
Optional additions: raisins, apple slices, or oat bran

Beat eggs, sugar, oil, vanilla, salt, cinnamon, soda, baking powder, and flour. Mix well. Add zucchini and nuts. Add optional ingredients, if desired.

Pour batter into greased loaf pans. Bake 40 to 60 minutes at 350 degrees F. Freezes and travels very well.

Old-fashioned Oatmeal Raisin Pancakes (serves 6)

½ cup raisins
2 cups oatmeal
¼ cup dry buttermilk
2 teaspoons cinnamon
2 tablespoons brown sugar
2 cups pancake mix

Mix together everything but the pancake mix. Add 2 cups water and stir. Let sit overnight.

Add the pancake mix in the morning, and stir until moistened. (Batter will be thick.) Cook on greased griddle.

For more recipe ideas see:
The Hungry Hiker's Book of Good Cooking, Gretchen McHugh. 1982.
Alfred A. Knopf, New York.

APPENDICES

Appendix A: Reference List

Appendix B: Pack Trip Pre-departure Checklist

Appendix C: Five-day Menu (with vegetarian options)

Appendix D: Llama Sales Contract and Bill of Sale

Appendix E: Quick-release Knot (drawings)

Appendix F: Parts of a Llama (drawing)

APPENDIX A

Reference List

LLAMA ASSOCIATIONS

International Llama Association (ILA)
Sandy Chapman, General Manager
P.O. Box 37505
Denver, CO 80237
phone: 303-756-8794

This is the largest llama association and offers monthly newsletters, membership directory, and an annual conference to members. The assoiation publishes free educational brochures on breeding, feeding, packing, herd management and health, available upon request to members and nonmembers.

Memberships are available for individuals, farms, and "affiliate members" (who pay a lower fee to receive the newsletter but not discounts at the annual conference).

Affiliated Organizations of the ILA: Alaska Chapter; Alpaca Owners and Breeders Association; California Chapter; Central States Chapter; Greater Appalachian Llama Association (GALA); Llama Association of Mid-Atlantic States; Llama Association of Southern California; Llama Owners of Washington State; Northern Rockies Chapter; Ohio River Valley Chapter; South Central Llama Association; Sunshine States Llama Association; Willamette Valley Llama Association.

The Llama Association of North America (LANA)
P.O. Box 1882, Dept. L
Minden, Nevada 89423
phone: 707-265-3177

LANA offers members a quarterly newsletter, membership directory, reference materials on llamas. General memberships and breeder's memberships (inclusion on commercial lists for advertising) are available.

This group promotes 4-H and Youth Llama Projects, sponsors annual educational and llama shows, and supports llama medical research.

Free educational brochure available upon request.

Canadian Lama Association
Chris McLachian, General Manager
Box 476
Bragg Creek, Alberta
Canada T0L 0K0
phone: 403-949-2955

International Lama Registry
Box 7166
Rochester, MN 55903
phone: 507-281-2178

This registry for all lamas is maintained by an independent, nonprofit organization.

Rocky Mountain Lama Association
25314 County Road T
Dolores, CO 81323

LLAMA PUBLICATIONS

Periodicals

Llama Life
2259 County Road 220
Durango, CO 81301-8019
phone: 303-259-0002

Quarterly newspaper with informative articles on both packing and breeding of llamas.

Llamas Magazine
P.O. Box 100
Herald, CA 95638
phone: 916-448-1668

Bi-monthly magazine, breeding and packing articles.

Canadian Llama News
Marie Lammle, Editor
6012 Third St., S.W.
Calgary, Alberta
Canada T2H OH9

Bi-monthly magazine.

The Backcountry Llama

2857 Rose Valley Loop
Kelso, WA 98626
phone: 206-425-6495

This newsletter contains articles specifically geared to packing. Published bi-monthly in even months.

Llama Link

Drawer 1995
Kalispell, MT 59903
phone: 406-752-2569

This free publication offers classified ads and services listings. February issue focuses on packing equipment.

Llama Catalog

International Llama Association
P.O. Box 37505
Denver, CO 80237
phone: 303-756-9004

The ILA publishes this free directory of llama products and services, including breeders, commercial packers, publications/videos, ranch equipment, and pack equipment. It is updated annually.

Books and Videos

<u>Training and Packing</u>

Barkman, Betty and Paul. 1989. *A Well-Trained Llama: A Trainer's Guide* and *Llamas in Their Formative Years: Behavior and Socialization.* 1991. Betty and Paul Barkman, 34190 Lodge Road, Tollhouse, CA 93667.

Bodington, Helen. *Llama Training on Your Own.* Polite Pets, 697 Fawn Dr., San Anselmo, CA 94960.

Burt, Sandi. 1991. *Llamas: An Introduction to Care, Training, and Handling.* Alpine Publications, P.O. Box 7027, Loveland, CO 80537.

Faiks, Jan and Jim, and Phyllis Tozier. 1985. *Llama Training: Who's in Charge?* Faiks' Alpaca and Llama Farm, P.O. Box 521152, Big Lake, Alaska 99652.

ILA Educational Brochures, ILA, P.O. Box 37505, Denver, CO 80237, 303-756-9004. Short brochures on feeding, llama facts for new owners, housing and fencing, wool, herd management, packing, and low impact camping with llamas.

Juniper Ridge Press (P.O. Box 338, Ashland, OR 97520; 1-800-869-7342) publishes books and videos on subjects including TTEAM training, driving, and packing. Among the titles available from Juniper Ridge Press:

Daugherty, Stanlynn. 1989. *Packing with Llamas.*

Hart, Rosanna. 1991. *Llamas for Love and Money.*

Hart, Rosanna. 1987 (rev. ed. 1991). *Living With Llamas.*

Markham, Doyle and Cherrie. 1990. *Llamas are the Ultimate* (training, feeding, packing, hunting, fishing, and care). Doyle and Cherrie Markham, 7626 N 5th West, Idaho Falls, ID 83402.

McGee, Marty. *Llama Training and Handling, The TTEAM Approach.* 1992, and *Basic TTEAM With Llamas* featuring Marty McGee (a video), 1992. Both are available from Marty McGee, 4251 Pulver Road, Dundee, N.Y. 14837, phone 607-243-5282, fax 607-243-5866. Marty can also provide information on TTEAM training clinics in your area. We highly recommend attending one of these clinics.

Taylor-Gavin Communications. *Let's Go Packing; Llama Basics, Breeding and Birthing;* and *All About Llamas* (videos). Taylor-Gavin Communications, P.O. Box 4323, Bozeman, MT 59772.

Tillman, Andy. 1981. *Speechless Brothers, the History and Care of Llamas.* Early Winters Press, Seattle, Washington. Unfortunately this book is out of print, but your library or a local llama owner may have a copy.

<u>Health Care and First Aid</u>

Hoffman, Clare, D.V.M. and Ingrid Asmus. 1989. *Caring for Llamas: A Health and Management Guide.* Rocky Mountain Lama Association, 168 Emerald Mt. Ct., Livermore, CO 80536. A resource book with illustrations of basic conformation plus health care instructions.

Lewis, Beth. 1986. *A Handbook for Llamas: First Aid Techniques.* Beth Lewis, 2780 Merlin Galice Road, Grants Pass, OR 97526. Short manual, including items in first aid kit and poisonous plants.

Morris, Joy, D.V.M. and Myra Freeman. 1990. *Llama First Aid for the Barn.* Sunshine States Llama Association Marketplace, Rt 1, Box 346, Lula, GA 30554. Short manual (26 pages).

Poisonous Plants

Fowler, Dr. Murray E. *Llamas Magazine*, January/February 1985 (then called *3-L Llama*). This article lists the signs of poisoning and the habitat in which you might find the plant.

Hoffman, Clare, D.V.M. and Ingrid Asmus. 1989. *Caring for Llamas: A Health and Management Guide*. Rocky Mountain Lama Association, 168 Emerald Mt. Ct., Livermore, CO 80536. The appendix contains a list of poisonous plants.

James, Wilma Roberts. 1973. *Know Your Poisonous Plants*. Naturegraph Publishers. Drawings and descriptions of plants poisonous to humans with associated signs and symptoms.

United States Department of Agriculture, *Plants Poisonous to Livestock in the Western States*. Agriculture Information Bulletin Number 415, U.S. Goverment Printing Office, Washington, D.C., 1980.

Walter, R., PhD. 1980. *Poisonous Plants*. Department of Botany and Plant Pathology, Colorado State University, Ft. Collins.

Camping

Fletcher, Colin. 1974. *The New Complete Walker*. Knopf Press, New York, NY. Covers backpacking equipment. For many years considered the bible of backpacking.

Greenspan, Rick, and Hal Kahn. 1985. *Backpacking: A Hedonist's Guide*. Moon Publications, Chico, California.

Hampton, Bruce, and David Cole. 1988. *Soft Paths*.. Stackpole Books, Harrisburg, PA. Great book covering all aspects of minimum impact camping and camping in bear country. Sponsored by NOLS, the National Outdoor Leadership School.

Herrero, S. 1985. *Bear Attacks: Their Causes and Avoidance*. Winchester Press, Piscataway, NJ. Gets into the nitty-gritty of bear psychology and ways to avoid an attack.

Kahn, Hal. 1991. *Camper's Companion: The Practical Guide for Better Outdoor Trips*. Foghorn Press, San Francisco, CA.

Manning, Harvey. 1986. *Backpacking: One Step at a Time*. Vintage Books, New York. Covers all the basics for the beginning backpacker.

Schneider, B. 1977. *Where the Grizzly Walks*. Mountain Press Publishing Co, Missoula, MT. This book is out of print but may be available at libraries or used book stores.

EQUIPMENT SALES

Rocky Mountain Llamas
Bobra Goldsmith
7202 N. 45th St.
Longmont, CO 80503
phone 303-530-5575

Packs, halters, general equipment. Catalog available.

Quality Llama Products
6615 SW McVey
Redmond, OR 97756
phone: 1-800-638-4689
phone: 503-548-5315

Packs, halters, general equipment. Catalog available.

Mt. Sopris Llamas Unlimited
0270 County Road 111
Carbondale, CO 81623
phone 1-800-484-4017 (TONE) 2681
303-963-3604

Packs, halters, general equipment. Catalog available.

Ecopack
Dave Harmon
P.O. Box 8342
Missoula, MT 59807
phone 406-542-1625

Soft-saddle pack system and packing clinics.

INSURING YOUR LLAMA

Some farm/ranch policies will include named perils insurance for livestock. Check with your insurance agent.

Aries Livestock Insurance
612 Park Avenue, Box A
Rich Hill, Missouri 64779
phone 417-395-2184 (in Missouri)
1-800-641-2072 (toll free outside Missouri)

Sterling Bloodstock Assurance, Ltd.
14 Martin Lane
Cherry Hills Village, CO 80110
phone 303-781-2199
fax 303-781-1710

Wilkins Livestock Insurers, Inc.
Box 24, Rural Route 1
Geneva, NE 68361

APPENDIX B

PACK TRIP PRE-DEPARTURE CHECKLIST

GENERAL GEAR
- ___tents, how many?
- ___ground cloths
- ___tarp
- ___rope for stringing tarp
- ___small shovel for latrine
- ___saw
- ___fire grill
- ___solar shower
- ___water filter

LLAMA GEAR
- ___stake-out pins, how many?
- ___stake-out lines
- ___extra halter, neck collar
- ___bug spray for llama
- ___grain
- ___mineral supplement
- ___feed & water buckets
- ___llama first-aid kit
- ___saddles with all rigging
- ___panniers
- ___lead ropes

KITCHEN GEAR
- ___trash bags
- ___hot pad gloves
- ___3 serving utensils
  (spatula, big spoon, ladle)
- ___can opener
- ___bulk matches
- ___salt and pepper
- ___frying pan
- ___stove grill
- ___flatware
- ___paper towels
- ___cloth towels
- ___cups
- ___water pot
- ___coffee pot
- ___cooking pot
- ___dishpan, dish drainer
- ___stove
- ___fuel hose for stove
- ___propane fuel
- ___plates, bowls
- ___dish detergent
- ___sponge/scouring pad
- ___sharp knife

DAY PACK GEAR
- ___compass, map
- ___full water bottle
- ___first-aid kit (human)
- ___survival kit
  - ___waterproof matches, fire starter
  - ___space blanket
  - ___dehydrated food
  - ___whistle
- ___toilet paper
- ___binoculars
- ___field guides
- ___camera, film
- ___lip balm and sunscreen
- ___bug repellent
- ___sunglasses

PERSONAL GEAR
- ___sleeping bag & pad
- ___face cloth & hand towel
- ___biodegradable soap
- ___toothbrush, toothpaste
- ___flashlight
- ___pencil & notebook
- ___reading material
- clothes:
  - ___underware for each day
  - ___a pair of socks for each day
  - ___a pair of long pants
  - ___hiking shorts
  - ___a couple of T-shirts
  - ___a warm, long-sleeved shirt
  - ___sweater (preferably wool)
  - ___long underwear
- footwear:
  - ___one pair hiking boots
  - ___one pair tennis shoes
- ___rain gear
- ___hats & mittens
- ___swimsuit
- ___jackknife

VEHICLE
- ___check tire pressure
- ___check oil
- ___check water level
- ___clean windshield

FOOD

APPENDIX C

Five-day Menu
(with vegetarian options)

DINNERS

1) Brazilian Black Bean Soup
   (*see recipe Chapter 11*)
   > Appetizer: chips and salsa
   > Main course: Brazilian Black Bean Soup
   > Serve with tortillas, sour cream & yogurt,
   >   salsa, refried beans-black dehydrated,
   >   chopped tomatoes, hot pepper jack
   >   cheese, lettuce
   > Dessert: brownies and fresh peaches

2) Szechuan Chicken with Stir-fried Vegetables
   (*see recipe Chapter 11*)
   > Main course: Szechuan Chicken,
   >   Stir Fry Vegies (zucchini, tomato,
   >   mushrooms, green onions)
   >   Rice (cook according to directions on bag)
   > Homemade bread
   > Salad: chopped cabbage
   > white wine
   > Dessert: rhubarb cake

3) Spaghetti
   > Main course: Spaghetti with pesto and/or
   >   tomato-based sauce (sautéd green
   >   pepper, garlic, and onion; tomato
   >   paste, spaghetti sauce seasoning packets)
   > parmesan cheese (in baggie)
   > Salad: chopped cabbage
   > Italian Herb Bread (two small round loaves)
   > Dessert: cheese cake (from mix)

4) Hot and Sour Tofu Soup
   (*see recipe Chapter 11*)
   > Swiss Cheese and Herb bread
   > Dessert: Zucchini Bread
   > (*see recipe Chapter 11*)

LUNCHES

1) Pre-made turkey and cheese sandwiches
   on rye bread (*see recipe Chapter 11*)
   > tomato, sprouts, pickles for sandwiches
   > apples
   > muffins

2) bread
   > peanut butter
   > jelly
   > cheese
   > tomato
   > cucumber
   > canned salmon
   > mustard
   > plums
   > cookies (fig bars)
   > snack crackers (cheese nips in baggies) for
   >   day hikes

3) hummus (from mix)
   > lemon (to add to hummus)
   > bread
   > peanut butter
   > jam
   > fruit
   > cookies

4) pita bread
   > sardines or salami
   > vegetable pate (canned)
   > cheese round (gouda or other variety)
   > rice cakes or crackers
   > dried fruit
   > cucumber
   > cabbage
   > banana bread (*see recipe Chapter 11*)
   > cookies

5) cheese
   crackers (wheat thins)
   peanut butter
   jelly
   sardines or salami
   cookies
   dried fruit

BREAKFASTS

1) French Toast with Eggs
   maple syrup (in squeeze bottle)
   bread
   butter
   jam
   yogurt (or sour cream left over dinner)
   4 eggs and ½ cup of powdered eggs

2) Old-fashioned Oatmeal Raisin Pancakes
   (*see recipe Chapter 11*)
   maple syrup
   butter
   jam

3) and 4) (2 mornings, alternate with hot breakfasts)
   Granola
   Instant oatmeal with maple syrup
   dried milk
   dried fruit
   banana or zucchini bread

APPENDIX D

LLAMA SALES CONTRACT

This sales agreement, dated the _____ day of _____, 199___, between Sally Selaur of Llama Ventures, Missoula, Montana, Seller, and Bob and Betsy Byer of Huson, Montana, Buyers, is for the sale of one male llama, VENTURE'S BORIS.

Parties agree as follows:

1) DESCRIPTION OF LLAMA:
Boris is a brown llama with white on legs, neck, and face and black on face. Boris was born September 6, 1991; Boris is registered with the International Lama Registry (ILR number 91111). His sire is McGruder and his dam is Lindy Miss.

2) SALES PRICE:
Sales price is _____ Dollars, payable as follows:
$100 deposit due immediately upon signing
$_____ balance due by _____ (date)___, or upon delivery. Seller will furnish a Bill of Sale for the total purchase price upon receipt of the balance due.

3) HEALTH WARRANTY: Seller warrants that Boris is in good health with no known defects or injuries. Seller will furnish Buyers with health records on Boris. If, between now and the time of sale, there is some change in the condition of the llama that would affect his ability to pack, the Seller agrees to refund the deposit.

4) VET CHECK, ADDITIONAL WORMING, OR FECAL TEST AT BUYER'S EXPENSE: Buyers agree to pay for any additional worming medicines, fecal exams, or vet examination which the Buyer may request be done on the llama prior to delivery. Seller will continue to provide routine worming and vaccinations at no charge. Buyer will be entitled to a full refund of the deposit and release from this contract in the event Boris is found by a veterinarian to be in unsatisfactory health or condition in a pre-purchase veterinary examination.

5) RECEIPT OF DEPOSIT AND FORFEITURE PROVISION: Seller hereby acknowledges receipt of a deposit in the amount of $100 from Buyers. In exchange for this deposit, Seller agrees to hold the llama until _____ (date)_____. Buyers agree that if the balance of the purchase price is not paid by _____ (date)_____, and the provisions of paragraph four (above) have not been met, Buyers will forfeit the deposit and Seller will be free to sell the llama to another party.

6) BOARDING FEES: Seller agrees to provide normal care and board at no charge until ____(date)_____.
After that date, board will be $30 per llama, per month, to be arranged by separate boarding agreement after Buyers have paid the balance of the purchase price.

7) COMPANION ANIMAL: Buyers realize the importance of companionship for a llama, and therefore agree to provide a companion animal (llama or other species) prior to accepting delivery of Boris. Buyers agree that if they cannot provide a companion animal for Boris, they will either board Boris at Llama Ventures or elsewhere where he will have companionship, or forfeit the deposit.

Signed and dated this _____ day of _____, 199___.

_____
Sally Selaur, Seller
Llama Ventures
P.O. Box 8342
Missoula, MT 59807

_____

_____
Bob and Betsy Byer, Buyers
P.O. Box 21
Huson, Montana 59834

BILL OF SALE

In accordance with the terms of the Llama Sales Contract dated ____(date)_____, Sally Selaur hereby sells the following llama to Bob and Betsy Byer of Huson, Montana:

The male llama is known as VENTURE'S BORIS (ILR #91111). Boris is a brown llama with white on legs, neck, and face and black on face. Boris was born September 6, 1991; his sire is McGruder and his dam is Lindy Miss.

Total purchase price for VENTURE'S BORIS is $_____ (_____Dollars), the receipt of which is hereby acknowledged.

Seller warrants that she is the lawful owner of VENTURE'S BORIS and that she has the right to sell the llama.

Date of sale: _____, 199____.

Signed: _____
        Sally Selaur, Seller

APPENDIX E

How to Create a Quick Release Knot

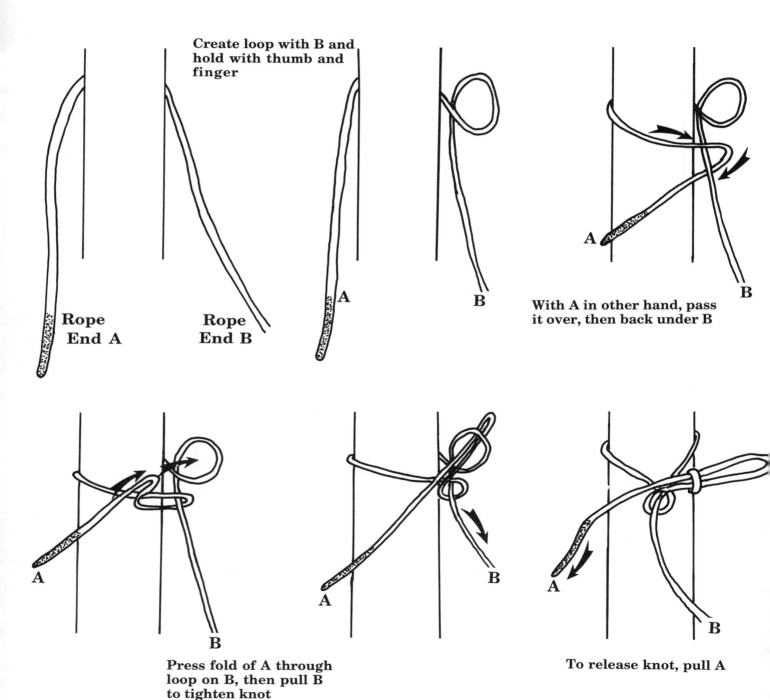

Create loop with B and hold with thumb and finger

Rope End A

Rope End B

With A in other hand, pass it over, then back under B

Press fold of A through loop on B, then pull B to tighten knot

To release knot, pull A

APPENDIX F

Parts of Llama

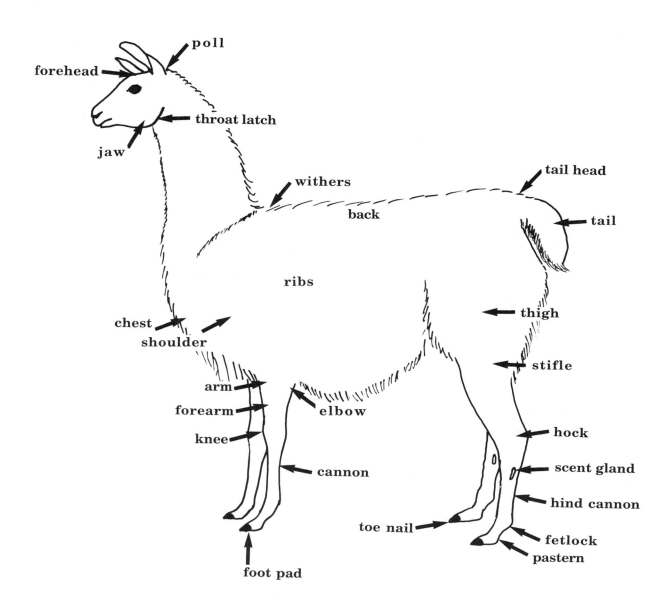

Index

Amy (left) and Dave (center) begin construction on their new barn, assisted by Amy's mother Joy Rubin.

About the Authors

David Harmon and Amy S. Rubin bought their first llama in 1986. They began breeding the animals and leading pack trips the following year. David founded Ecollama Wilderness Treks, combining his love of the outdoors with his background in natural history to lead hikers on wilderness packing trips. Amy owns and manages Llama Ventures, breeding a herd of female llamas for packing qualities. She also contributes behind the scenes to Ecollama pack trips with gourmet meals and advertising. The couple offer packing clinics every spring for beginning llama packers and instruct National Forest Service personnel on the proper use of llamas in the backcountry. Both David and Amy contribute regularly to *Llama Life* magazine. The couple live in Missoula, Montana, with their fleet of over two dozen llamas.